Peaks a̶

Integrative Approaches for Recovering from Loss

By
Sherry O'Brian,
LCSW, NBCCHt, DCEP

Ⓒ I know the weekends will be hard for you now — hopefully this will guide you...

OZARK
MOUNTAIN
PUBLISHING

Library of Congress Cataloging-in-Publication Data

O'Brian, Sherry – 1957

Peaks and Valleys by Sherry O'Brian

Powerful tools to transform and recover from any kind of loss and reawaken to the possibility of joy.

1. Loss 2. Grief 3. Death 4. Self-Help

I. O'Brian, Sherry, 1957 II. Grief/Loss III. Title

Library of Congress Catalog Card Number: 2014937979

ISBN: 9781940265049

Cover Design: enki3d.com

Book set in: Times New Roman, Century Schoolbook

Book Design: Tab Pillar

Published by:

PO Box 754

Huntsville, AR 72740

800-935-0045 or 479-738-2348 fax: 479-738-2448

WWW.OZARKMT.COM

Printed in the United States of America

Dedication

This book is dedicated to my sister, Jeanne; my parents; the memory of my nephew, Shane; my brother, Larry; and all those who have endured a devastating loss.

Endorsements

"This beautiful book weaves together Sherry O'Brian's clinical wisdom and personal experience with grief. With insight and compassion, she helps the reader deal with pockets of unresolved emotions using powerful energy therapies so a person can move through loss into reorganization and recovery."

Barbara Stone, author of *Invisible Roots: How Healing Past Life Trauma Can Liberate Your Present* and *Transforming Fear into Gold*

"Sherry O'Brian's *Peaks and Valleys* book is a well-constructed, clear work on how to deal with grief and loss. Rather than a rehash of traditional methodologies, O'Brian takes a cutting edge approach, based in science, and offers plenty of excellent exercises, examples and stories to help the reader make practical use of the material. There is no doubt this excellent book will help many sufferers of grief and loss to find their way back to a more balanced, enjoyable life."

Pamela Bruner, Business Coach, EFT expert and co-author with *Jack Canfield* of *Tapping into Ultimate Success: How to Overcome any Obstacle and Skyrocket your Results*

"Sherry truly is a transformational author. Her Peaks and Valleys book provides the reader with powerful tools to transform and recover from any kind of loss. These tools go beyond traditional methods of recovery to help readers move through their pain and discover a life of love and joy on the other side."

Christine Kloser, The Transformation Catalyst, Three-time Award Winning Author, Creator of The Transformational Author Experience program

"Change is the only constant. But we are wired to hold on to what we have loved, to what was known and familiar. Therein lies much of our suffering since change always involves the loss of what was, making the way for what will be. Sherry O'Brian has written a wonderful guide for navigating our way through the peaks and valleys that accompany the changing landscape of our lives."

Donna Eden and David Feinstein
Co-Authors, *The Energies of Love*

Acknowledgments

I would like to thank my family and friends for believing in me and my ability to write this book.

To my husband, Pat: Thank you for your patience during this project.

To Betsy Muller and Meda Killgore: Thanks for sharing your experiences as authors as well your friendship.

I want to thank Donna Voll for planting the seed about my writing a book so many years ago. I would also like to thank Christine Kloser and her Transformational Author Experience program, which became the catalyst for actually completing this book.

Next, I would like to thank Mike Silver and Donna Pittman for giving me permission to share his story and her poems.

I also want to thank all of my bereavement group members, clients, and workshop participants for allowing me to share their personal healing journeys and requesting that I place this information into a book format.

I would like to thank all of the pioneers in the field of energy psychology and Energy Medicine—Roger Callahan, Gary Craig, Donna Eden, David Feinstein, Patricia Carrington, Barbara Stone and many others—for without this training, none of this book would have been possible.

In addition, I want to thank Donna Eden and Innersource for allowing me to reprint a version of Donna Eden's Daily Energy Routine.

In addition, I thank the Association for Comprehensive Energy Psychology for their pioneering work in advancing the field of energy psychology and allowing me to share this information at their annual conferences.

I would like to thank all of my wonderful teachers and mentors in the mental health field; I especially thank David, Diane, and Yvonne with The Wellness Institute for my healing/training in hypnotherapy and subtle energy.

I would also like to thank God and all those who are no longer with me in body but will always be with me in spirit—for giving me clarity when I had none and understanding the importance of sharing this book.

Finally, I would like to thank Karen Wilczewski at Top Dog Communications, the first editor of this book. Without her willingness to help me with this project, this book would not have been nearly as nice to read.

Table of Contents

Preface

Within this book, you will be introduced to several cutting-edge integrative modalities, which are currently supported by ongoing research. Although several of these techniques have been around for thousands of years, these modalities have not been extensively researched by Western medicine and psychological communities. For more information or further research on the various techniques presented here, please visit: www.energypsych.org and follow the links provided. For additional information on any authors mentioned in this book, please refer to the References and Recommended Reading section.

The tools shared in this book are not meant to replace professional counseling or medical treatment. Neither the author nor the publisher will be responsible or liable for any loss or damages arising from any of the information or suggestions presented in this book. Do not stop taking any prescribed medication without first consulting your health care professional even if you feel the medication is no longer necessary.

Please enjoy these tools of transformation with an open mind and heart.

Introduction

Many losses go unrecognized or are subtle—some are life changing. Whether you have lost a loved one, a relationship, or a job, the energy of grief often weighs heavily upon your heart, making it difficult to enjoy life after a loss. Nevertheless, loss is often misunderstood and is frequently prevalent among those suffering from chronic illness and other life experiences. Grief is both an emotion and a process. If grief is left untreated or unacknowledged, its effects can accumulate, causing psychological blocks that may interfere with one's ability to enjoy life. Today it is more important than ever to understand the process of recovery from loss, as many individuals struggle with unemployment, loss of a home, individual lifestyle/status, loved ones, and so forth.

Loss is unique because *all* individuals will eventually experience it in some form or other. Whenever there is any kind of attachment, if the bond or connection is broken, a loss cannot be avoided. Even when this disconnect is beneficial, such as recovery from addiction, a loss can occur. The loss of friends, family, activities, and coping behaviors that were once acceptable are now severed.

When an event occurs that destroys our understanding of the meaning of life, our beliefs and expectations come under attack, and we experience loss. Dreams may fade away as we age, goals may become unattainable, and a sense of loss can occur. Physical limitations, illnesses, and disabilities may create a sense of loss. Such losses may be gradual or sudden. Unfortunately, many individuals are unaware they have experienced a loss. Therefore, they ignore or deny the emotional process of grieving, and the energy of these emotions becomes "frozen" within. As these emotions accumulate, they can cause each subsequent loss to be even more difficult to process. This book is designed to help the reader release the burden associated with loss and once again awaken to the joy in life.

In Part 1, I discuss various types of losses and perhaps shine some light on those losses that often go unrecognized. A brief overview of the different theoretical perspectives on grief and loss is shared, as well as some of the myths associated with these perspectives.

In Part 2, I provide the reader with an overview of the mind/body/spirit connection among those suffering from grief and loss. This is designed to deepen the reader's understanding of this connection and provide a framework for addressing this distress, using the various techniques presented in Part 3 of this book.

In Part 3, the reader will be taken on a journey of transformation, using the integrative tools of Energy Psychology, Energy Medicine, rituals for healing, guided imagery, and meditation. I have successfully used these tools in various forms with my clients, workshop/retreat participants, and on myself to transcend the energy of grief and loss. For more information on these workshops and retreats, please visit my website at www.mindbodyspirit-innergrations.com.

Throughout this book, you, the reader, will be asked questions to deepen your experience of the material discussed. Therefore, I encourage you to use a journal or notebook to record this information. I will also share exercises in which this information will be used to assist you on your journey of transformation.

As a psychotherapist, I often notice my clients experiencing unresolved grief and loss associated with several psychological issues. However, it was when tragedy struck my family that I began the journey of deepening my understanding of loss and assisting others and myself, using the various techniques I outline in this book. The stories woven into this book are true. The names have been changed or omitted to protect the individuals' identity and to provide confidentiality. My hope is that the reader will find solace in the stories and recovery in the process using the methods I share. I am honored and humbled by those who choose to embark on this journey with me as we navigate the peaks and valleys of grief and loss.

Part 1:
An Exploration of Loss

The griever's suffering is never constant... Each peak represents a mountain of pain, each valley a restful lull. Initially, the peaks are high and long, the valleys are narrow and short, and the frequency is high. Slowly, the peaks mellow, the valleys lengthen and the frequency decreases.

--H. Norman Wright

1

Chapter 1:
Death, the Final Goodbye

Thought of you with love today, but that is nothing new. I thought of you yesterday, and days before that, too. I think of you in silence; I often speak your name. All I have are memories and a picture in a frame. Your memory is a keepsake with which I'll never part. God has you in his keeping. I have you in my heart.

--Unknown Author

It was one of the worst snowfalls of the season when I got the call—my 21-year old nephew had died from his battle with cancer. I wasn't sure how I would get there—my sister lived in the country, and the roads were already bad. However, I knew I needed/wanted to be there with her and with him one last time. As my husband and I drove through the blizzard-like conditions, I prayed and remembered a few days earlier—the last time I said goodbye to my nephew. He was struggling so to stay awake and apologized for nodding off. I didn't mind. He was in so much pain towards the end of his life as he struggled to breathe that it was a comfort to know he could escape through sleep. To this day, I'm not sure how we made it to my sister's house; I suspect Divine Intervention. The next memory of my nephew was seared forever into my mind.

As I walked into his room, I saw my sister lying beside my nephew on his bed, cradling her son in her arms for the last time. I felt helpless. All my training as a psychotherapist and bereavement counselor fell away as I witnessed a mother's sorrow—my sorrow. There was nothing I could say. In the silence, I could feel my sister slowly slipping away as if she were willing her very soul to join her son's. I was led to do some energy work with her to ground her back into her body once again. I now understood firsthand what my clients' refer to as feeling "as though a piece of them was being ripped away" upon the death of their loved ones.

We sat in silence and held this sacred space with prayer and ritual to assist my nephew's soul—our souls. This vigil lasted until my sister was ready, and the coroner arrived. It was a powerful reminder of the healing power of ritual. I had no idea at the time how often I would call upon this power—six months later, my youngest brother committed suicide.

Suicide: The Shameful Loss

No one knew the torment that you were going through.
We only kept on seeing what we really wanted to.

We saw the outward smile but not your inner pain.
We never really dreamt that you would never smile again.

Forgive us if we failed to see what we could do to aid,
Or if we failed to comprehend how much you were afraid.

We pray your mental anguish will now forever cease
And that your deep anxieties will be replaced by peace.

We know your pain invaded every single thought you had.
It made you cry internally and be deeply, deeply sad.

But we in turn remember the good times, not the bad.
We remember when you smiled at us and not when you were sad.

So when we think about your life, we won't dwell upon its close.
We'll remember all the good times and forget about life's blows.

We'll remember all the happiness, the joy and not the tears,
The assurance and the confidence, and not irrational fears.

Our lives have all been better because you have been there,
So now we leave your memory in God's all-loving care.

--Unknown Author

Once again, I vividly remember the day I received the call that my brother had shot himself. I remember feeling shocked and angry. My brother had made several attempts prior to his last one, and each time I tried to assist him in any way I could. The last time I spoke to him I remember seeing the desperation and pain in his eyes; however, he assured me that he would call me before attempting anything again. He did not.

As I made my way over to my parents' house (he was living with them at the time), I could only imagine what they must be going through. When I arrived at the house, the police were already there, and it felt like something out of a movie. I tried my best to console my parents, but once again, there was nothing I could say. However, I knew I needed to help my brother one last time. I asked the police if I could have some time with him. I entered his room with the intention of helping him cross over and say goodbye. It was one of the most difficult rituals I would ever perform, but something in me knew it was necessary for him and for me.

When we lose a loved one as a result of suicide, we are often referred to as "survivors." I've come to understand this term both personally and professionally. The shame, anger, and remorse became unbearable at times; after all, I was a professional and should have been able to help my brother!

Survivors are in a precarious position—angry at the victims, yet loving and missing them. If the victim has made multiple attempts, survivors may even feel *both* a sense of relief and subsequent guilt. Grief becomes confusing and complicated and is often very traumatic. Therefore, the trauma often must be dealt with before the grieving process can begin.

The traumatic loss of a loved one can be any sudden, unexpected loss, from murder to a catastrophic event. Although it is often referred to as sudden, unexpected, or tragic, I've also seen the loved ones of cancer patients who died from their disease experience similar emotions. However the loss occurred, it is the *response* to the loss that qualifies it as traumatic. I will cover this in more detail in Part 2 of this book, but for now, let's look at some of the common characteristics associated with this type of loss.

Survivors often lose their sense of safety. Flashbacks of the event may occur. There may be an ongoing sense of feeling numb or in shock. They may feel a sense of confusion about their role in life. And life as it once was perceived is forever changed. These are just a few of the experiences one may suffer as the result of a traumatic loss.

Perhaps you are also experiencing some of the above-mentioned characteristics. If so, know that the trauma you experienced can be transcended with perseverance and a willingness to practice the tools set forth in this book. I will share more about the mind/body connection related to trauma, as well as how it impacts the grieving process in Part 2 of this book. Part 3 will address techniques to help you transform trauma.

Other Forms of Death/Loss

When a couple loses a child from a miscarriage, often it is difficult to grieve the loss. There are no social traditions within our culture to help with this type of loss—no funerals, memorial services, or ways to acknowledge the loss. However, it is, in fact, a loss, and oftentimes multiple losses of this kind occur. With each subsequent loss, the grief becomes even more difficult to cope with. Therefore, it is important to recognize *each* miscarriage as a loss and grieve it accordingly. I had a client who lost her eight-month old son to spina bifida. After a few years, she and her husband tried to have another child but continued having miscarriages—each triggering unresolved grief from the initial loss of their son that was compounded by each additional miscarriage. We used the tools in Part 3 of this book to help her sort out her grief and begin the healing process.

Another frequently overlooked loss is abortion. Now I know this is a highly-charged issue, and it is not my intention to take sides. However, abortion is a loss and is comparable to suicide, leaving the survivors with feelings of shame and guilt. Often this loss goes unrecognized until much later in life. However, sometimes the grief is experienced immediately, and depending on the circumstances, the woman is left to grieve on her own. The father may also grieve and feel that his child was murdered. In terms of both parents, if this loss is not processed properly, it can complicate any further loss, as well as affect many other issues in life.

Journal Activity

For now, allow yourself to think back to when you lost someone you love; it can also be the loss of a pet. Be gentle with yourself, but be aware of the emotions you experience. As you recall this loss, write down your memories as they are part of your story. I will share more about the healing power of story in Part 3 and share tools to assist you in transcending the pain.

Chapter 2:
The Subtle and Not-So-Subtle Losses

The older I get, the more invisible I become in a culture where youth and external beauty reign. All the while I've become more beautiful to myself because I am embracing and honoring the wisdom that my life experiences have brought and the kindness, compassion and tenderness that grief and loss have engendered.

--Julie Daley

Dreams may fade as we age, goals may become unattainable, and a sense of loss can occur. Physical limitations, illnesses, and disabilities may create a sense of loss. These losses may be gradual or sudden. As we age, we experience many losses that go unrecognized—loss of abilities, job/retirement, sense of identity, and so on.

As children, we go through developmental stages, each having its own set of losses—childhood fantasies, school friends, relationships, teachers, mentors, and so forth. Each stage is a transition in and of itself, and although some religious cultures recognize these milestones, most do not. Therefore, without honoring that which is lost, we risk unresolved grief later in our adult lives.

When I was sixteen years old, I decided that I wanted to get married, have babies, and "live happily ever after." I married my first husband at sixteen and had my son two days before turning seventeen. I grew up fast. My childhood fantasy was shattered. I worked hard just to survive. I lost my childhood and my dreams; however, I was not aware of this at the time. I was divorced at age twenty-one and became a single parent— another loss. It was not until recently that I fully understood the ramifications of those early losses. I had to grieve my losses in order to learn how to play and enjoy life once again.

The loss of any significant relationship, whether through divorce or loss of a friendship, can cause considerable grief. This often involves many relationship changes and the loss of an entire support network. In addition, routines and roles change. If the loss is from divorce, often children are involved, and parents must grieve along with their children. Then there are also secondary losses: financial, home, dreams, and so forth. This lifestyle change impacts the entire family.

We are often told that we must prepare for retirement by saving and investing our money. However, many of us fail to prepare for the loss associated with retirement. We may lose friendships, as well as a sense of structure to our lives. Some of us lose our sense of identity and self-confidence when we retire. I had a client come in for weight loss issues, and as we explored this further, a self-esteem issue surfaced.

I asked, "When was the last time you felt good about yourself, in control, and self-assured?"

He shared how much he enjoyed the work he used to do and how it gave him a sense of purpose. He described how he missed the action involved in his job and how he was able to remain calm during challenging times while on the job. As we continued to explore this, it became obvious that he had not recognized retirement as a loss, and, as a result, he had not fully grieved this loss.

In my workshops, I often demonstrate how our identities or lack of them can create this dilemma. I ask the audience to do the following exercise. I encourage you, the reader, to try it as well.

Journal Activity

- Jot down on a piece of paper who you are as if you are writing your autobiography. Now, look at what you have written.

In my workshops, I ask for a volunteer to read or share this exercise with other audience participants. Most individuals will usually share what they do for a living (i.e., social worker, psychologist, etc.) and sometimes relate their roles as a mothers, fathers, wives, husbands, etc., for this is how we define often ourselves in this society. I then challenge them by asking—who would you be if all of this disappeared? My workshop participants found it very challenging to do this exercise.

- Now try describing yourself without the roles you play.

Historically, as individuals, we could call upon myths and stories for direction or guidance during these life transitions. However, in our modern day society, we have lost the power of story. We no longer have or use the myths and stories of our ancestors to guide us through life's difficult transitions. In the book *Navigating the Future* by Mikela Tarlow, the author suggests, "We are in trouble personally and culturally because we lack transitional stories. We don't have myths that can take us from one set of beliefs to another." Any transition or change in life can result in a loss. Without sufficient guidance, our losses can compound. This accumulating loss can make each subsequent one more difficult to transcend. I will discuss the power of story and ritual in Part 3 of this book as one way to assist you with using this powerful form of healing.

A chronic or life-threatening illness encompasses several types of loss. While facilitating a cancer support group, I began to notice several losses associated with this disease. For example, a man diagnosed with breast cancer described his inability to carry a bag of salt to his water softener because of weight restrictions. He had been an avid motorcycle rider, as well as a gun owner, and he could no longer participate in either activity. He explained the associated feelings and his sense of loss related to his identity as a man and the loss of many of the activities he enjoyed in life. Others in the group related to his sense of loss as they recounted all the secondary losses that had occurred as a result of their diagnoses and the various side-effects of treatment. The loss of body parts, pleasure, identity, intimacy, hope, a job, self-esteem, mobility, and so on. Each of these losses was difficult to mourn because it was not recognized as loss. Once diagnosed, cancer patients and their loved ones often experience what is referred to as "diagnosis shock"—life as it once was is now forever lost.

Unfortunately, many individuals are unaware they have experienced a loss. Therefore, they ignore or deny the emotional process of grieving, and these emotions become "frozen" within them. If a loss is not recognized or fully processed, any subsequent loss may reactivate the feelings of loss associated with it. For example, I was working with a woman who lost her husband after he battled cancer. She was in a difficult situation at work with a boss who was very demanding and had unrealistic expectations. This caused a decrease in her appetite, difficulty sleeping, racing thoughts, and anxiety. She described how angry, helpless, and hopeless she felt when I suggested she stop for a moment and go back to another significant time in her life when she felt similar emotions. Needless to say, these were the exact emotions she experienced as she watched her husband slowly die from cancer—anger, anxiety, helplessness, and hopelessness. These emotions had been reactivated once again by her current work experience. Armed with this awareness and some of the tools that will be shared in Part 3 of this book, she was able to process this grief and became empowered to move through these emotions and make the necessary changes in her life.

Another often overlooked loss is experienced when a loved one is stricken with Alzheimer's disease or some other form of dementia. Although the person is still alive, he or she is no longer fully present. There is no memorial or other service to acknowledge this loss. Relationship roles are changed, intimacy is lost, and entire families are forgotten. I have seen the loved ones of these individuals re-traumatized with each visit. Furthermore, for the spouses of these individuals, moving forward seems impossible. As a result, a paralysis or sense of limbo occurs.

Similar losses are experienced when family members are reported missing. Years may go by with no information forthcoming about their loved ones—they have simply disappeared. Often, no funerals or memorials are held—just a sense of limbo and difficulty moving forward.

I know there are many other forms of loss that I have not covered here. However, my intention is to assist you to recognize your own unique forms of loss. Perhaps there are subtle (and not so subtle) losses you have experienced that have gone unrecognized.

Journal Activity

- Do you or someone you love suffer from a loss of mobility or other abilities?
- Have you recently retired?
- Have you lost a job?
- Are your goals or dreams fading away?
- Have you lost a significant relationship?

In your journal write down your experience, thoughts, feelings, and any insights you may have. We will use this information in Part 3 of this book to assist you to transform your pain into possibility.

The Grieving of America

We plan our lives according to a dream that came to us in childhood, and we find that life alters our plans.

--Ben Oki

An entire group of people can experience loss. We have seen and heard of job losses occurring within our economy. As a result, individuals lose their homes, status, lifestyle, dreams, and identity. Communities are grieving. When an event occurs that destroys our understanding of the meaning of life, our beliefs and expectations come under attack, and life as we once knew it is gone forever. We saw this play out on September 11, 2001, when our whole community and the world came together in our shared grief over the losses that occurred. Even if we were not personally touched by those losses, we were affected and effected by them. The loss of our personal freedoms is an additional loss that resulted from increased security around the world. The devastating losses from war, hurricanes, tornados, and so forth have impacted this country and other countries more than we know. All of these losses add up, and they create an energetic field woven with the underlying threads of grief and loss.

Scientists are beginning to measure and document the power of a community's influence as a whole on each individual member. There are several theories for this phenomenon although all of them explain it from a slightly different perspective. Rupert Sheldrake refers to this as "morphic resonance" and explains it this way: ". . . similar things [energetic vibrations] influence similar things [energetic vibrations] across both time and space. The amount of influence depends on the degree of similarity." In other words, the community's energy resonates (or doesn't resonate) with us and vice versa. Sheldrake further explains that societies or communities "can function and respond as a unified whole via the characteristics of its morphic field." A "morphic field" is created by a shared belief or perspective, a consensual view of the world and reality; when this reality is shattered, so too is its identity. Many individuals and communities are now struggling with this loss of identity.

Social scientists have studied similar aspects of this phenomenon. One way is looking at the influence of a group on individual behavior. For example, an individual may react or behave differently alone than within a group. Often referred to as "groupthink" or group consciousness, the energy of the group can often influence an individual's decision. Historically, we have seen the shadow side of group consciousness (to be discussed further later in this chapter) within Nazi Germany and elsewhere. Recently, scientists have actually been able to look at the energy field that is created by this group consciousness. For more information on this research, I recommend visiting The Global Consciousness Project's website listed in the reference section and the other authors' websites or books mentioned in this section.

As a path of perception (or belief) is created, so, too, is its "morphic field." All those who follow this path contribute to it. You can see this pattern in professional groups, as well as other types of communities. There is a consensus within these groups about how problems should be solved and how reality operates. This is often referred to as a "paradigm." Therefore, a paradigm shift involves not only a new way of solving problems but also a new consensus view of reality. This is why paradigm shifts are often rare and usually meet with a great deal of resistance.

We are witnessing this currently within our society. From healthcare reform to the banking industry, the morphic fields of these groups are being challenged, upsetting their morphic resonance, and thus the status quo within these communities. This is being experienced as a loss within the community though it is not recognized as such. Therefore, this grief has accumulated individually and collectively within our communities, and until it is recognized, our communities will continue to grieve and recovery cannot occur.

In *The Field: The Quest for the Secret Force of the Universe*, by Lynne McTaggart, the author suggests that our consciousness can and, in fact, does affect what she refers to as "the field." This field is defined as "a subatomic field of unimaginably large quantum energy in so-called empty space." This field "connects everything in the universe to everything else, like some vast invisible web." Gregg Braden refers to this field as the "Divine Matrix."

Regardless of what this field is called (morphic, Divine, or field), when enough individuals develop a consensus view of reality, this field will be created or impacted in some way. For example, if we remain in a consensus of fear and grief within our communities, then we hold the morphic field (or group consciousness) for this experience to continue. However, if we hold the consensus of hope and transformation within our communities, then this will be our experience. Currently, I believe that several of our communities are stuck in the shock and protest phase of the Grief Cycle, which I will discuss in more detail in the next chapter.

Our perceptions of reality may be challenged as our society continues to shift from old paradigms and make way for new experiences. However, if we avoid the fear of change and allow ourselves to grieve our losses, we might experience a new reality and identity within our community. I will share more tools on how to accomplish this in Part 3 of this book.

Another similar but often overlooked or misunderstood form of grief is ancestral grief. If you remember, I have suggested that whole communities can grieve as a result of group consciousness. The morphic field of groups, such as the American Indians, African Americans, the Jewish community, and so on, have endured mass trauma. This trauma is held at a cellular level within the human body and within the energetic field or group consciousness of these cultures. Other generations within these communities can continue to hold this energy of grief for generations to come unless it is recognized and released at a cellular level.

For example, I had a client who was struggling with depression. Upon questioning her, I realized that she was describing unresolved grief; however, she was unaware of any particular loss. Without going into all the details, I used hypnosis to help her find the source of her grief. She went back to a time when her ancestors were being slaughtered. We resolved this at the source and freed her energetic connection to it.

I will discuss this in more detail in Parts 2 and 3 of this book; however, for now, start thinking about your ancestral lineage. Perhaps you can identify which, if any, ancestor carried this type of traumatic grief. It does not have to be specific to a group or culture; however, the grief is often much stronger if it is.

Journal Activity

Here are some questions to ask that may assist you in determining if you are holding onto your ancestors' or community's grief:

- Where do I focus my thoughts?
- What is the consensus of reality within my community?
- Is this consensus sabotaging or supporting me?

- Are my beliefs congruent with the community I choose to associate with?

- As paradigms continue to shift and new information is presented, do I resist and stick with the status quo?

- Do I recognize and mourn my losses?

- Do I remain open to embracing a new identity/reality?

- Did my ancestors undergo severe trauma?

- Do I suffer from an unexplained sense of loss?

Divine Homesickness

When we are constantly focused on externals, we are not centered, that is, we are not aligned internally—body, mind and soul. Without that alignment, we have a case of Divine Homesickness. We feel empty and lost, always trying to find our way Home . . . always looking for something 'out there' to fill us up. And nothing out there can.

--Susan Jeffers

Another often unrecognized form of grief is referred to as "Divine Homesickness," a profound sense of loss from or connection with the Divine. Some individuals have difficulty remaining "fully present" and find themselves either intentionally or unintentionally disassociating from life. Often, life seems too difficult to deal with, and there is a deep longing to return to the spirit world. For other individuals this may be characterized as an attempt to fill a void with other inappropriate relationships in life, thus, placing the burden on another to satisfy their spiritual longing. There may be a sense of abandonment or feelings of not fitting in as if they belong somewhere else.

In an article in the Desert News titled "Defending the Faith" Daniel Peterson (2012) wrote about these feelings of not fitting in. He said, "I believe that such experiences offer powerful religious meaning to those who've had them. They are, I think, *stabs* of *divine homesickness*, a yearning for something unspeakably and unchangingly beautiful, good, and holy."

Peterson shared the feelings of Eliza Snow, William Wordsworth, and the poet Rumi on this subject. Eliza Snow reminisced that even before Mormonism, "Oft times a secret something whispered, *You're a stranger here*, and I felt that I had wandered from a more exalted sphere."

William Wordsworth perceived "intimations of immortality" (and of a pre-mortal existence) in nature.

Peterson (2012) continued, "The Persian poet Rumi compared the human soul to a reed; the plaintive sound of reed pipes expresses the reed's longing for its lost home in the reed bed just as we yearn for the divine home from which we've been severed."

However, I believe healing can occur if we approach this existential issue of Divine Homesickness as a grief recovery process. In *Chronic Grief–Spiritual Midwifery: A New Diagnostic and Healing Paradigm* Gowell Childs wrote: "As the roots of the Chronic Grief are systematically addressed and the turbulence, i.e., the chaos in the system is addressed, the sufferer has fewer and fewer episodes of distress, and grief, and more joy."

I have used hypnotherapy, as well as the tools I share in Part 3 to assist individuals with becoming aware of and healing this issue. For example, I worked with a woman to assist her in reconnecting with the Divine/God internally rather than as an external relationship in which she felt the only way to connect with God was within an altered state of consciousness. You, too, can use the various tools I have provided to assist you with reconnecting and releasing this type of grief and distress.

Journal Activity

Here are some questions to ask that may assist you in determining if you are suffering from Divine Homesickness. Once again write down any insights or information you may have. We will use this information in Part 3 of this book to assist you in transforming this pain.

- Do you find that you have trouble staying fully present and have a tendency to daydream or disassociate often?

- Do you have an unexplained sense of loss or feelings of abandonment?

- Do you have difficulty fitting in and feel lost or alone?

- Do you find yourself attempting to fill a void with inappropriate relationships?

- Do you have an excessive preoccupation with meditation or some other form of creating an altered state of consciousness?

Now that we have explored several types of loss, I invite you to review the list (See Table 2.1) that follows. Please know this is not meant to be an all-inclusive list but rather a catalyst to assist you in perhaps recognizing some of the losses you may have forgotten along the way. Refer to this list often and add to it as you begin to recognize other losses you have experienced in your life. Remember: with awareness comes recovery Next we will explore the myths often associated with grieving and recovering from these various types of loss.

Types of Loss

Death of a Loved One	Job/Retirement
Relationships	Home
Mobility/Abilities	Dreams
Identity	Beliefs/Meaning in Life
Status/Life Style	Faith/Divine Homesickness
Pet Loss	Other losses

Table 2.1

Chapter 3:
Breaking the Stages of Grief Myth

Grief is an intense set of emotional reactions in response to a real, imagined, or anticipated loss.

--Linda J. Schupp
Is There Life After Loss?

There are many models of the grief process; however, one of the most well-known is the "stages of grief" model by Elizabeth Kubler Ross. The stages include denial, anger, bargaining, depression, and acceptance. The Elizabeth Kubler Ross model was originally developed while working with terminally-ill patients, and it was not meant to be adapted to the bereaved. Unfortunately, it is still taught in various schools and hospice organizations as the standard bereavement model. I find that this model can confuse the bereaved because it implies that if we go through the various stages of grief, we can expect to *complete* or *finish* the process. I believe this is one of the most misunderstood processes of grief. Although we can learn to live with our losses, most of our losses are not forgotten, nor should they be.

Another model that I believe is more appropriate for the bereaved is known as The Four Tasks of Mourning, which appears in *Grief Counseling and Grief Therapy, Second Edition,* by J. William Worden, Ph.D. These four tasks are:

1. Accepting the reality of the loss;
2. Working through the pain;
3. Adjusting to the environment; and

4. Emotionally relocating the deceased, that is filing away in a safe place the mental and emotional memories of the deceased.

This model is specific to the loss of a loved one, but again, it implies a stage or step-like fashion that we go through after a loss.

Therefore, one of the models that I find most helpful when working with individuals who have experienced any kind of loss is referred to as the Grief Cycle (see Figure 3.1). This cycle consists of shock, protest, disorganization, reorganization, and recovery. I want to emphasize that these are *phases*, not stages that one moves through after a loss. Moreover, there is no time limit on grief, and although there are common issues that most individuals face after a loss, we each will move through these phases at our own pace.

Figure 3.1 The Grief Cycle

The Grief Cycle represents the natural movement of emotions that we go through in the recovery process:

- the shock of the loss;
- the subsequent protest of the loss;
- the feeling of disorganization as a result of the loss;
- the redefining of self as reorganizing occurs; and
- the recovery process.

All are part of this cycle. Keep in mind that we can and often do continue to move through these phases several times during our recovery process.

Obviously, the most devastating loss is that of a loved one. However, the process of recovery is much the same, albeit far more intense. As we navigate through the cycle of grief, we will ultimately experience the peaks and valleys of emotions associated with our loss. Regardless of the loss, in order for recovery to occur, we must go through the feelings associated with the loss. There is no way around this. If we suppress these feelings, they can ultimately cause physical, psychological, and/or emotional disorders. Numerous studies have indicated that we are more susceptible to heart attacks, cancer, and other illnesses after the death of a loved one or any other significant loss. However, it is *how we respond* to the stress of the loss, not the actual loss, which determines our susceptibility. If we reach out for guidance on our journey through the various phases of the grief cycle, this susceptibility lessens, making way for our growth and recovery. Gradually, as healing occurs, this journey becomes less intense and less frequent.

As you read through each of these phases, I will ask you a series of questions at the end of each section to assist you in processing the information you discover. Please write your responses in your journal. The tools I share with you in Part 3 of this book will help you on your journey through the various phases of the Grief Cycle. This information will assist you in using the various techniques to transform and transcend any energetic blocks that may be sabotaging your recovery. For now, let's look at how each phase of the Grief Cycle may apply to your individual loss.

Shock

The shock phase is the initial reaction we experience with the discovery of a loss. Often a sense of disbelief or denial occurs in this phase. We may feel emotionally numb. This acts like a shock absorber, allowing us to gradually comprehend that a loss has occurred. We often see the shock phase shortly after the death of a loved one, such as at funerals. Family and friends gather round and function on what has been described as "auto pilot." There is often a surreal feeling associated with this experience. Others may experience anger at what has happened as a way of dealing with the sense of helplessness that often occurs in this phase. Regardless of the loss—whether it is a loved one, a job, a relationship, and so forth—if there is an attachment of any kind, a sense of shock will occur.

Journal Activity

Consider the following questions. I will cover more about the importance of treating the trauma that often occurs in this stage in Part 2 of this book; however, for now, just get in touch once again with your unique experience of the loss and write it down in your journal.

- Can you recall feeling a sense of shock related to a loss in your life?

- What was this experience like for you? Perhaps you are still in this phase. If so, tune into the feelings (or lack thereof) to get a better sense of your experience.

- Are you revisiting this phase? If so, are you aware of what triggered it for you?

- Are you reliving a loss in your mind?

Protest

The protest phase usually occurs when the suffering is fully acknowledged. These feelings can become intense and often depend on the severity of the loss. The "why" questions are frequently a part of this phase—why me, why them, why now, and so forth. An attempt to find meaning in the loss is often a part of this phase of the grief cycle. Our core beliefs and values are often challenged, and our sense of the world and our place in it comes into question. Often many adjustments are made as a result of the loss—looking for a new job, a change in roles, new tasks that must be learned, and so on. This can feel overwhelming because all of this may be experienced along with various emotions, such as fear, anger, anxiety, sadness, helplessness, hopelessness, and so forth. Our physical endurance, along with our sense of self, is often compromised during this phase of the grief cycle.

Journal Activity

Ask yourself the following questions. Just be aware of your experience/s and avoid judging it/them as right or wrong and write in your journal what you are aware of:

- Have you experienced, or are you currently in the protest phase of the Grief Cycle?
- Do you find yourself asking why?
- Are you feeling overwhelmed by the tasks at hand?
- What emotions are you aware of?
- Have you lost your sense of self?
- Are your beliefs and values being challenged?

Now let's move on the next phase of the grief cycle.

Disorganization

The disorganization phase of the grief cycle is experienced when despite our protests and attempts to find meaning in our loss, life as it once was seems to disintegrate. Our coping skills may come into question as feelings of being overwhelmed rise, and familiar routines no longer work. Everyday habits and routines are usually impacted by a loss and can be experienced as secondary losses. A loss of identity and a sense of self often continue to come into question during this phase. Roles come into question, and perhaps new roles are forced upon us. Frequently, our support system(s) can disintegrate. The individuals we reached out to in the past for support are either unavailable or unable to fully understand what we are going through. We can feel very vulnerable during this phase.

Journal Activity

Consider the following and respond in your journal.

- Have your familiar routines and habits changed as a result of your loss?

- If so, how is this affecting you on a daily basis?

- Have your roles changed as a result of your loss?

- Has your support system changed or disappeared?

Reorganization

The reorganization phase of the grief cycle begins when a new sense of self, apart from that which was lost, occurs. New habits and routines are created that provide us with a sense of stability. Perhaps new support systems have been created that provide a new sense of self. We develop coping skills that provide us with a sense of strength as feelings of helplessness dissipate. However, we will continue to question this new sense of self and life until a new sense of equilibrium occurs. If we have lost loved ones, we may experience a sense of guilt and shame during this phase. Fear of forgetting a loved one or shame about moving forward can interfere with our recovery process throughout this phase.

Journal Activity

Here are some helpful questions to ask yourself during this phase:

- How can I feel safe again?
- What do I remember most about _____?
- What do I enjoy?
- Who am I apart from _____ (your loss) _____?
- What can I do without_____?

The journey through these various phases is progressive. You may continue moving through each phase more than once before moving closer to the recovery phase. This is the process of recovery—moving through the various phases. When our movement comes to a halt, this is when we need-assistance.

Recovery

The recovery phase of the grief cycle implies learning to live apart from and in spite of the loss. It does not refer to "getting over" or completing the grief process. If we have lost a loved one, we will never come to a point where we no longer miss that person. However, we can learn to live with this grief in such a way that it no longer incapacitates us. This phase, like all the others, is fluid in nature, and we may pass in and out of it, as well as the other phases in the recovery process. It is for this reason that I placed The Recovery Phase in the middle of the Grief Cycle (see Figure 3.1). Anniversaries or other milestones will often trigger us to revisit a particular phase of the Grief Cycle. This is normal and part of the grief process. The ebb and flow of the other phases of the Grief Cycle all evolve around and include the recovery phase.

Journal Activity

In your journal, respond to the following questions:

- Am I trying to return to my former life?

- Am I reinvested in life?

- Have I achieved a new sense of meaning and purpose in my life?

- Can I remember the good things about what I have lost without becoming overwhelmed by the pain?

- Do I have an anniversary or other milestone coming up?

There are, of course, other models of grief and loss; however, I find this Grief Cycle model to be more applicable to several forms of loss. Now that you have a basic understanding of how this model works, we will begin exploring how we can become stuck in a particular phase. To do this, we need to delve more deeply into the mind/body/spirit connection.

Therefore, in Part 2, I will share the basic science behind how we experience our emotions within our bodies, not just our minds. The aspect of trauma within the grief process will be discussed. I will also share information on the various energy systems within the body and how they are affected by a loss. My hope is that all of this information will help facilitate your understanding of why the tools shared in Part 3 can be so powerful when perhaps others have seemed to fail.

Part 2:
It's All Connected – Mind, Body, & Spirit

Our bodies contain our histories—every chapter, line and verse of every event and relationship in our lives.

--Carolyn Myss
Anatomy of the Spirit

Chapter 4:
Trauma Is in the Eye of the Beholder

At the frontiers of research of the mind, scientists are suggesting that every cell in your body has some capacity to remember; and that failure to consider and treat "body memory" accounts for the continued power of a psychological trauma.

> --Sheila Sidney Bender, PhD and Mary T. Sise, LCSW
> *The Energy of Belief*

What is trauma? Trauma can be experienced when we have undergone or witnessed a traumatic event that involved an actual or threatened death or serious physical injury to ourselves or another. As a result, we felt intense fear or helplessness. The symptoms often associated with trauma include flashbacks of the event(s), hyper-arousal, numbness, amnesia, intrusive thoughts, sleep problems, difficulty concentrating, depression, and so forth.

Our brains are "wired" to protect us from life-threatening events. The limbic system is part of the brain that helps us assess this level of threat and primarily consists of the amygdale and hypothalamus. The limbic system is activated during times of severe stress or life-threatening events; this is often referred to as the flight/fight/freeze response. The problem often occurs when we cannot escape the threat/situation, and a freeze response happens. If there is no way to discharge or release this energy, it literally becomes frozen within the body and brain. The threat or perceived threat is re-experienced, creating a feedback loop or chemical cascade within the body and brain even when there is no longer any real danger present. It is this response to past events as if they were happening now that characterizes trauma.

Therefore, trauma truly is in "the eye of the beholder." If we feel this level of threat, regardless of the circumstances, an actual chemical response within the body and brain can and does occur. If we have experienced trauma, we may have more difficulty recovering from our loss until the trauma itself is treated and released at the cellular level. I have witnessed this among the loved ones of cancer patients and cancer patients themselves. For example, I noticed a common theme while working with those whose loved ones died of cancer. They would share difficulty remembering their loved one without recalling the last few days, weeks, or months of watching them suffer from the treatment and the disease. They would often describe having flashbacks of these memories and difficulty sleeping, problems concentrating, and so forth. They would say they felt helpless—unable to "save" their loved ones from certain death.

Vicarious trauma is another form of trauma. It refers to an inner transformation of a caregiver's experience, resulting from repeated exposure to and empathic interaction with another's traumatic material. These effects are often seen among healthcare practitioners. The effects are cumulative and often permanent, impacting both their personal and professional lives.

There are certainly different levels of trauma among those who have suffered a loss. Losing a job, a relationship, a body part, and so on can also be traumatic. Each depends on how the loss is perceived as to whether or not trauma will be experienced. The important point here is that trauma keeps an individual stuck in the past. Each time a trigger or cue is experienced, an eruption of old unreleased or unsolved memories can occur.

Journal Activity

In Part 3 of this book I will share various tools to assist with releasing this trapped energy. My intention here is to simply create awareness. One way to do this is to ask yourself the following questions and write your answers in your journal. As you gather this information, know that you are also picking up the pieces that will assist you to release and recover from your loss. This information will be used on your journey of transformation in Part 3 of this book.

- When you think about your loss, do you have difficulty remembering the "good times"?

- Do you have flashbacks of the event(s) that occurred prior to or during your loss?

- What emotions or feelings did you experience during this time?

- Do you have any of the symptoms associated with trauma: flashbacks of the event(s), hyper-arousal, numbness, amnesia, intrusive thoughts, sleep problems, difficulty concentrating, depression, and so forth?

Now as we move into the next chapter, we will explore how the body's energy system actually holds this information both at a cellular and energetic level. We will also explore why we often must intervene at this level for recovery to occur.

Chapter 5:
An Exploration of the Body's Energetic System

When you eventually see through the veils to how things really are, you will keep saying again and again—"this is certainly not like we thought it was.

--Rumi

The next big frontier in medicine is energy medicine.

--Dr. Mehmet Oz

The Chakras and Biofield (Aura)

Before we begin exploring the various tools of transformation, I want to share a brief overview of the body's energy system. Some of you may already be familiar with the concepts of the chakras, meridians, and the aura (biofield) of the body. However, to better understand why some of the tools I will be sharing with you in Part 3 are so effective, I recommend that you review the following information. For those of you who are new to these concepts, I encourage you to keep an open mind as we delve into the various explanations and subsequent research related to them. It is not my intention to provide an all-inclusive overview of the research here—rather, simply to introduce you to these concepts. For more information, please see the References and Recommended Reading section of this book.

As science evolves, so too does our understanding of the body's energetic system. What was undetectable by science at one time can now be seen and measured. One of the first tools used to measure the human biofield or aura was Kirlian photography (see Figures 5.1a and 5.1b). Photographing the biofield (aura) was developed in the 1930s and demonstrates that every living thing is surrounded by an energy field. The biofield (aura) is an electromagnetic field that surrounds our entire body. It (see Figure 5.2) contains a person's energy, protects against harmful environmental energies, and helps us to connect with others. This field is affected by changes in our emotions and physical states. It acts as a filter for life energies. Think of white light passing through a prism (our biofield). When it does, the light is divided into different vibrational frequencies and is then distributed to various organs of the body through the chakras.

Figure 5.1a

Figure 5.1b—Aura pictures from Kirlian photography. The aura is
affected by changes in our emotions and our physical states.

The word "chakra" is taken from the Sanskrit word meaning
"wheels." Chakras (see Figure 5.2) resemble whirling vortices
of subtle energy. The chakras are involved in transmuting
higher vibrational energy into a usable form. This energy is
then utilized by the body's endocrine and nervous systems.
Because of this interconnection, any dysfunction within the
chakras can create pathology within the nervous system. This
dysfunction within the body's energetic system can act as an
impasse or block within the system, making it difficult to
release or discharge any emotions frozen within the body. The
tools presented in Part 3 of this book are designed to release
these frozen emotions. Now, let's take a closer look at the
body's energetic system.

Figure 5.2 Chakras and Aura

In Figure 5.2, you can see the various chakras, each represented by a color. Each color represents the velocity in which the chakra vibrates. Dr. Hunt and associates studied the effects of Rolfing, measured the frequency of these signals from the body, and mathematically analyzed the wave patterns. Their results showed the following color frequency correlations (Hz = hertz or cycles per second):

- blue = 250-275 Hz;
- green = 250-275 Hz;
- yellow = 500-700 Hz;

- orange = 950-1050 Hz,
- red = 1000-1200 Hz;
- violet = 1000-2000 Hz;
- white = 1100-2000 Hz.

These results are remarkably consistent with ancient texts' descriptions of the chakras.

The crown (7th) charka is located at the crown of the head and is usually represented by the color white. The brow (6th) chakra is located just above the center of the eyebrows and is sometimes referred to as the third eye and is often represented by the color violet. The throat (5th) chakra, located mid-throat, is represented by the color blue. The heart (4th) chakra, located mid-chest, is usually represented by the color green. The solar plexus (3rd), chakra is located on the upper stomach region, and represented by the color yellow. The sacral (2nd) chakra, located in the mid-abdominal area, is represented by the color orange, and lastly, the root (1st) chakra, located at the tailbone or end of the spine, is represented by the color red.

Please keep in mind that these are generalizations and may vary, depending on several factors that include a far more advanced study of the chakras and is beyond the scope of this book. My intention is to provide you with a general understanding of the chakras. As I indicated earlier, the chakras resemble whirling vortices of subtle energy. When a chakra is open or is operating correctly, each vortex rotates clockwise—transforming energy into a useable form. The tools I share in Part 3 of this book will teach you how to ensure that each chakra is open, balanced, and operating properly. Next we will look at the meridians within the body and the role they may play in recovery from loss.

Meridians and Acupoints

The meridians act as another means of transporting subtle energy, sometimes referred to as "chi," throughout the body. When there are blocks or disruptions within any of the meridians, this energy ceases to flow properly and can prevent any emotion(s) connected with the corresponding block from being discharged. Now let us briefly explore each one of these meridians and the acupoints involved in the exciting new field of energy psychology.

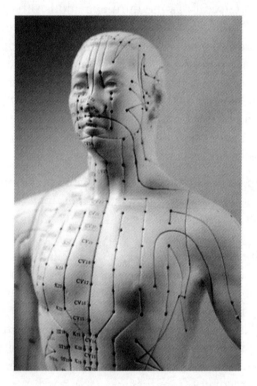

Figure 5.3—the Meridians and Acupoints

There are fourteen major meridians (see Figure 5.3) in the human body. These are the bladder, gall bladder, stomach, governing vessel, central vessel, kidney, spleen, liver, lung, large intestines, circulation/sex, heart, small intestines, and triple warmer. The acupoints are access points along each meridian. Dr. Y. King Liu researched acupoints and discovered they correspond to regions where several "nerve terminal elements" are located. There are several studies involving acupuncture; however, most of these studies are centered on pain management, which has been shown to work 70-80/% of the time. However, more recent studies involving energy psychology have also shown promising results for releasing emotional pain.

The basic premise of most energy psychology techniques is that one can discharge a blocked or disturbed energy pattern by stimulating specific acupoints on the body while the individual focuses on the upsetting issue. I explained the trauma response in Chapter 4; however, here is a brief excerpt to help explain it once again:

The limbic system is part of the brain that helps us assess this level of threat and consists mainly of the amygdale and hypothalamus. The limbic system is activated during times of severe stress or life threatening events; this is often referred to as the flight/fight/freeze response. The problem happens when one cannot escape the threat and the freeze response occurs. If there is no way to discharge or release this energy, it literally becomes frozen within the body and the brain. The threat or perceived threat is re-experienced creating a feedback loop or chemical cascade within the body and the brain even when there is no longer any real danger.

Therefore, by stimulating certain acupoints on the body, which are believed to deactivate specific signals within the amygdale (that occurred during an upsetting or traumatic event), physical and psychological changes can occur.

This is a brief overview of the field of energy psychology, which is one of the tools that will be presented in Part 3 of this book. It is not my intention to provide all of the research on this subject—rather, a brief explanation of how/why these techniques may assist you to recover from loss. For more information on the corresponding research, please refer to the References and Recommended Reading section. I have shared my personal and professional experiences with the hope they may help the reader in some small way. I have used each of the tools that I share in Part 3 to assist myself and others in navigating the journey through grief and loss. Now let us begin.

Part 3:
Integrative Tools to Transform and Transcend Grief/Loss

We will never understand the scientific basis of everything. We must be open to approaches that work even when we don't understand how or why they work.

--Ralph Snyderman

To change the printout of the body, you must learn to rewrite the software of the mind.

--Deepak Chopra, M.D.
Perfect Health

Chapter 6:
Mending a Broken Heart:
Creating Heart Brain Coherence

Grieving allows us to heal, to remember with love rather than pain. It is a sorting process. One by one you let go of things that are gone and mourn them. One by one you take hold of the things that have become a part of who you are and build again.

--Rachael Naomi Remen

It is only with the heart that one can see rightly, what is essential is invisible to the eye.

--Antoine de Saint-Exupery

The remaining chapters of this book involve using the various tools and techniques in conjunction with the information you have gathered from previous chapters. Please keep in mind that these tools may require you to use them several times to experience the desired results. In this chapter, I share a meditation that I created, "Release and Transform Burden: a meditation to awaken the healing light within," which is available for separate purchase on my website: www.mindbodyspirit-innergrations.com.

The heart is the most powerful source of electromagnetic energy in the human body. As people learn to sustain heart-focused positive-feeling states, the brain can be brought into entrainment with the heart. Heart-brain coherence is vitally important when we are recovering from loss. According to The Institute of HeartMath, the heart communicates with the brain and body in four ways: neurological communication (nervous

47

system), biophysical communication (pulse wave), biochemical communication (hormones), and energetic communication (electromagnetic fields). For our purposes, we will be focusing on the biophysical and energetic ways that the heart communicates with the brain.

When we have incurred a loss, one of the areas of the body that often holds the energy of this loss is within the heart. For example, when a loved one has died, we may know logically that we could not have prevented this loss, yet we feel as if maybe we could/should have done something differently. In this case, often the heart and brain are energetically incoherent. Thus, for healing to occur, it is important that coherence between the brain and heart once again be accomplished. The following exercises are just a few methods for accomplishing heart-brain coherence.

Holding Your Heart in Mind Exercise

First, find a comfortable position. You can do this exercise lying down or sitting up. Make sure you minimize any distractions. Take a few deep breaths and center yourself by focusing on your breath.

Now, when you are ready, slowly place your right hand over you heart chakra (mid-chest) and bring all your awareness to the palm of your right hand. Just notice the palm of your right hand.

Now bring to mind something you really love. All that is needed here is your attention and the intention to feel a pulsating or throbbing form of energy in the palm of your right hand.

Just take your time. With practice, you will become more aware of this energy pulsating in your right palm.

When you are aware of this energy, slowly place your left palm over your third eye (on your forehead slightly above the middle of the eyebrows) with your fingertips resting slightly on your head.

Now bring all your awareness to your left palm and again with your attention and intention slowly begin to notice a pulsation in your left palm. Again, just take your time.

When you are aware of the pulsing in your left palm, bring your attention once again to the pulsing in your right palm. Your intention is to synchronize the pulsing between the right and left palms of your hands.

Again, take your time. All that is required is your attention and intention.

When you experience this synchronization, simply place your hands in a prayer position in front of your heart center with your intention to lock in this energetic flow.

You are now experiencing heart-brain coherence.

Should you wish further instructions, there is also a video on my website: www.mindbodyspirit-innergrations.com, which will walk you through this exercise.

The Heart Massage Exercise

The following exercise is a wonderful way of releasing blocked energy from the heart. This exercise also works with the energies of the heart chakra; however, because it involves the energy of the heart, I have decided to include it in this chapter. For more information on the chakras, please refer to Chapters 5 or 9. For a visual representation of this exercise, please refer to Figure 6.1.

Place your right hand on your heart chakra (mid-chest).

Now gently and slowly massage this chakra in a clockwise motion (move your hand towards your little finger).

While massaging your heart, repeat an affirmation such as "Even though a part of me is having difficulty forgiving myself (or another), I am willing to try."

Also, include an affirmation that addresses any difficulty with loving yourself, such as "Even though I am having difficulty loving myself, I am now willing to accept myself unconditionally with all my faults."

You can also include any affirmation that would address difficulty letting go and being open to receiving.

Remember to trust this process and let go of whatever thoughts or emotions come to you during this exercise. Acknowledge the thought or emotion and affirm your desire to accept yourself anyway.

Figure 6.1

Meditation Exercise for Heart-Brain Coherence

This next exercise is a meditation that can be used to create heart-brain coherence, as well as balance all chakras in the body. I have placed it in this chapter, but it is an exercise that could easily fit into other chapters as well. The following meditation is the written script of my CD. I recommend listening to the CD, "Release and Transform Burden: a meditation to awaken the healing light within" for maximum results. However, if you choose to do this on your own, I recommend that you record this script for your personal use only.

Before we begin, I would like to familiarize you with the various energy centers (chakras) of the body. See Chapters 5 and 9 for more detailed information on the chakras and aura (biofield).

The crown chakra is located at the top (crown) of the head; it is associated with transpersonal awareness or spiritual connection. The brow chakra, sometimes referred to as the third eye, is located on your forehead slightly above the mid-point of the eyebrows and is associated with insight and seeing clearly. The throat chakra is located mid-throat and is associated with self-expression. The heart chakra is located mid-chest and is associated with compassion and forgiveness. It is important to note that the heart's electromagnetic field is 50 to 100 times more powerful than the brain's, and this energy can be felt up to several feet away from its source. Often it is within the heart center that the accumulation of emotion can become frozen, which, in turn, creates a ripple effect among the other energy centers or chakras.

The next energy center is often referred to as the solar-plexus or the third chakra. It is located on the solar-plexus (upper stomach region) and is associated with a sense of power and self-esteem. The sacral chakra is located mid-abdominal area, right below the navel—it is associated with choosing, manifesting, and sexuality.

The root chakra is located at the tailbone or base of the spine and is associated with survival and safety needs, as well as vitality and joy. Lastly, the biofield or aura is located all around the body and consists of several layers; however, the most important thing to remember here is that it embraces the body and acts as a protective field all around it. Every living thing has a biofield.

Now that you have a basic understanding of the energy centers within and around the body, let us begin.

Release and Transform Burden Meditation

First, find a comfortable place where you can relax. Turn off your cell phone, etc., and put the Do Not Disturb Sign out for others to see. This is your time. Give yourself at least thirty minutes of uninterrupted space. Once you become familiar with this meditation, you can certainly modify it to meet your individual needs.

For now, get into a comfortable position, close your eyes, and begin taking a few deep breaths.

Now with your next inhalation, hold your breath for a few seconds.... Now gently exhale and imagine exhaling all your tension.... Any worries you may have just float out with each exhale.

Now take another deep breath and hold.... As you exhale, begin to feel a wave of relaxation moving from your lungs into every cell of your body.

Take in one more deep cleansing breath and hold...As you release, feel your muscles relaxing and releasing with each exhale.

Now continue taking slow, relaxed breaths.... As I count from 5 to 1, slowly bring your attention to your heart center. Notice any images or sensations you experience here... Perhaps there is a sense of heaviness or cloudiness here... a sense of sadness or betrayal.... Just notice without judgment....

Now imagine you can see, sense, or feel a small silvery white light within the center of your heart.... You might imagine this as a beautiful star in the darkness of your heart... or perhaps the sun peeking out from behind the clouds.... Use whatever image that resonates with you....

Now allow this silver white light to get even brighter and increase in size.... as you release any darkness you may be holding on to...any blame of yourself or another ... any shame .... This is your soul's Divine essence.... Let it shine through.

Some refer to this as "the seat of the soul"....See this light getting brighter and brighter as you continue to release. Know that this is Divine love made manifest within you.... Before the burdens, before the trauma, before the grief overshadowed this light, it existed.... No one can take this from you.

Now see this silver white light in all its brilliance releasing any remaining darkness within your heart center and returning it to its Divine perfection....

When this feels complete, imagine sending this light to your solar plexus by spiraling it downward to the right from within.

Remembering the power of your heart to release and transform any blocks that may exist here....healing any false perceptions of self...with the light from your heart... and claiming a healthy sense of self....

Release any and all power struggles you may have with yourself or another....

Release all of those times when you felt completely powerless.

Claim your Divine power now!

Feel, sense, see the light within growing to fill up and transform this energy... releasing any and all blocks from your solar plexus now....

When this feels complete, imagine sending this light to your throat chakra by spiraling it upward... feel, sense, or see this powerful silvery white light from your Divine essence within your throat chakra now.... You may sense a sort of tickling in your throat as this energy begins to awaken.... It's okay to cough, clear your throat, or breathe out your mouth to assist this energy in clearing and releasing any stagnate energy here....

Continue to release any blame or judgment here....

Perhaps you can imagine all of the times when you felt you must refrain from speaking for fear of punishment... or times when you felt unheard....

Just see the light of your heart burning away any darkness or heaviness here... returning this center to its Divine perfection once again...

Allowing room for healthy self-expression... become more aware of the power of your authentic voice once again.... Know that your words have the power to create... see your throat center filled with the light of your heart now....

When this feels complete, imagine spiraling this silvery white light to your sacral chakra (mid-abdominal area); notice any blocks here perhaps around choosing or manifesting... any fertility issues... just notice again without judgment or blame, just see, sense, or feel the light spreading the unconditional love from your heart ... releasing any darkness, any blocks here, just slowly dissolve and transform....

If there are any issues around letting go of things you cannot control or change, often they are held in this area... just imagine the light of your heart releasing, forgiving, transforming this energy....

Now when this feels complete, send this silvery white light spiraling upward to the third eye—located mid-forehead, right above the brows—again observe without any judgment and notice any blocks that may exist here....

Perhaps some fear about the future or difficulty seeing any future at all... or memories of the past continue to haunt you... just allow the light of your heart to enter and dissolve away any illusions that may exist, allowing you to see clearly....

Release and transform any darkness and awaken your innate ability to see, to intuitively know what is in your highest good....

When this feels complete, send the light of your heart spiraling down to your root chakra, located at the base of the spine. Again, notice without judgment any blocks that may exist here... often, this may involve fear of survival...the lack of desire or will to live... or perhaps the inability to experience joy... just notice and see the light of your heart spreading and assisting you to release any darkness, heaviness, any burdens that you may have been carrying for yourself or another...dissolve into the light.

Notice the light gently transforming this energy back into its Divine perfection once again....

Now, when this feels complete, send the light of your heart to your crown chakra at the top of your head.... Just notice this, again without judgment. Is there a sense of disconnection from your Divine source? There may even be a sense of anger towards God... perhaps feelings of unworthiness or a sense of betrayal... see the Divine light of your heart opening this space once again.

Release any feelings or beliefs that would block you from your Divine source.... You and only you placed these here... know you need do nothing to deserve God's love... you have always been and will always be connected to source .... Release and transform any blame that may exist here...release any blocks or darkness that may exist here now....

Let the light of your heart strengthen your connection with the Divine essence of pure love once again....

Now when this feels complete, imagine sending this silvery white light from your crown, spiraling all around your entire aura (biofield) to assist you in releasing any remaining energetic contagions within your field.... Just imagine seeing, sensing, or feeling this light embracing you, repairing any rips, tears, or holes within your field....

Just notice the light continuing to spiral up and around you now.... All the way up to your higher self... and continuing upward toward the angelic realm and beyond...to the Divine where you release any remaining blocks and all that you have gathered on your healing journey....Know the power of this transformation...the Divine and angelic community applaud you and embrace you with unconditional love.... You are now ready, open, and willing to receive....

See this Divine healing energy now spiraling down around and upon you, now entering your crown chakra...flowing and spiraling down to the root chakra... from here to the third eye or brow chakra.... Continuing to spiral down to the sacral chakra...from here spiraling up to the throat chakra... spiraling down from the throat to the solar plexus...spiraling up from the solar plexus to the heart....

Now feel this energy filling your heart with unconditional love from the Divine... and take your right hand and place it on your heart center (mid-chest).... Feel this heart energy pulsating in the palm of your right hand.... When you are ready, slowly place your left hand on your brow chakra with your fingers cradling the scalp of your head.... Now notice the pulsations within your left palm....

Begin to notice the pulsations within both hands and synchronize these now. This may take some time—just know your intention to do this is all that is required. Now when this feels complete...slowly bring the fingertips of both hands together to lock in this energy.... You can do this hold any time you want to...the "holding your heart in mind hold" will assist you in maintaining coherence between your brain and heart... as well as remember your healing journey.

Now take a few deep breaths... begin to notice the time and place you are experiencing.... Become aware of your body... the chair or place you are sitting or lying.... Take in a few more deep breaths and imagine energy coming up through the soles of your feet, up the legs into the root chakra and all the way up the back of the spine and back down the front of the spine into your legs and out the soles of your feet, completely grounding you. When you are ready, slowly open your eyes and return to this time and this place....

Now may you continue to experience the light from within your heart.

Namaste

Chapter 7:
Tap into the Story:
Acupoint Stimulation for Healing

By choosing your thoughts, and by selecting which emotional currents you will release and which you will reinforce, you determine the quality of your light. You determine the effects that you will have upon others, and the nature of the experience of your life.

--Gary Zukav

Letting go of the emotions that trap you, painful memories, fears, depression, or anger, is the way to a longer and healthier life

--Deepak Chopra, M.D.

Acupoint Stimulation for Healing

Remember that energy psychology addresses what is believed to be disruptions in the human energy system by tapping, holding, or otherwise activating various acupressure points and energetic centers of the body. In Chapter 5, I shared that these and a variety of other techniques are designed to stimulate and balance neurological and systemic disorganization. As I said previously, "When there are blocks or disruptions within any of the meridians, the energy ceases to flow properly and thereby prevents any emotions connected with the corresponding block from discharging." The techniques I share in this section involve a basic tapping formula referred to as

Emotional Freedom Technique (EFT). We will explore only the basic short-form version of this technique although I have added some additional acupoints that I have found to be helpful when working with grief and loss issues. Please refer to Figure 7.1 for a visual representation of the points that will be used.

I encourage you to gather the information that you have been writing down in your journal from Parts 1 and 2 of this book. This information may help you to identify the beliefs that may be blocking you from your recovery process. Now pick one issue or emotion that you have gathered from this information. Tune into and become aware of how disturbing or distressful this specific issue or emotion makes you feel on a scale from zero to ten with zero indicating no significant disturbance or distress and ten being the most extreme disturbance/distress. This is referred to as your SUDS level—Subjective Units of Distress/Disturbance, and it will assist you in monitoring your progress.

The following exercise will focus on the particular acupoints that I have found to be the most important for stimulating an emotional release or clearing loss-related issues. However, please keep in mind that there are additional points that other energy psychology modalities use, including the long form of EFT. Moreover, when I work individually with clients, we can often zero in on the specific points that are involved with a specific issue. Therefore, I recommend this basic recipe to begin with, and if at any time your SUDS level increases rather than decreases, please seek professional assistance.

After you have determined your SUDS level, you will create an affirmation that addresses the issue(s) you want to work on. This will not be your typical affirmation; rather, it will address the issue or problem you want to work on using the following format:

"Even though a part of me has this (state issue or problem), I deeply love and accept myself anyway, even this part of me."

You can modify this statement, if necessary. For example, "Even though a part of me has this (state issue or problem), I deeply and completely accept this part of me."

The more specific this statement, the better. Repeat this statement aloud three times while rubbing the Sore Spots or tapping on the Karate Chop point (See Figure 7.1) on the side of your hand.

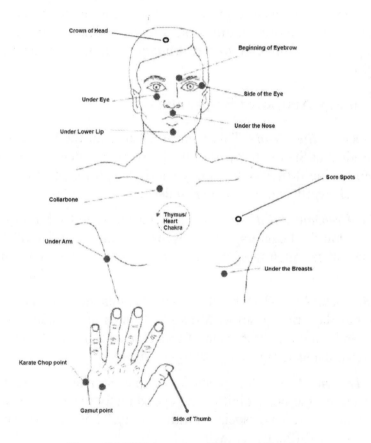

Figure 7.1 EFT Acupoints (Shortened Version)

Now, create a reminder phrase—a shortened version of the previous statement. For example, if the issue you want to work on is guilt, the full statement might look something like this: "Even though a part of me feels guilty about how I treated my brother before he died, I deeply love and accept myself, even this part of me." Now the reminder phrase is just a shortcut of this statement, such as the word "guilt." You will use it as a reminder of what you are working on as you tap (stimulate) each acupoint. You will tap each acupoint (See Figure 7.1) approximately seven-to-ten times as you repeat the reminder phrase. For more information on the location of each acupoints, please refer to the Primary Acupoint section that follows.

Primary Acupoint Sequence

Crown of the Head—This point is located on the Governing Meridian at the top (crown) of the head and is often associated with having difficulty trusting your Higher Power, feelings of low self-worth and/or of being punished.

The Eyebrow Point—This point is on the Bladder Meridian, located at the beginning of the eyebrow near the bridge of the nose. It is often associated with trauma, frustration, and restlessness.

Side of the Eye—This point is on the Gallbladder Meridian, as well as the Triple Warmer Meridian, located at the side of the eye and temples. When both of these are stimulated, they help to release anger, rage, and feelings of stress.

Under the Eye—This point is on the Stomach Meridian, located on the bony orbit of the eye, directly under the pupil. This point is often associated with anxiety, phobias, obsessive worry, and difficulty letting go.

Under the Nose—This point is on the Governing Meridian, located directly under the nose in the crevice between the nose and upper lip. This point is often associated with feelings of embarrassment, internal conflict, and lack of courage to move forward in one's life.

Under Bottom Lip—This point is on the Central Meridian, located directly under the bottom lip between the lip and chin. This point is often associated with feelings of shame, guilt, and vulnerability.

Collarbone Points—This point is on the Kidney Meridian, located directly under both collarbones. This point is often associated with feelings of anxiety, fear, and shock.

Thymus/Heart Point—This point is on the Central Meridian and actually works with the heart chakra and thymus gland. It is located in the center of the chest (see Figure 6.1) and can be stimulated either by thumping gently with the fist or by massaging (see the heart massage in Chapter 6) in a clockwise direction. This point is often associated with feelings of vulnerability, low self-worth, inability to forgive, and grief/sadness.

Under Arm—This point is on the Spleen Meridian, located on the side of the body about four to six inches under the armpit. This point is often associated with feelings of anxiety, negative self-esteem, toxic beliefs, and cravings.

Under Breast (Optional)—This point is on the Liver Meridian, located directly under the breast in alignment with the nipple, approximately where the ribcage ends. This point is often associated with unhappiness and toxic beliefs.

Karate Chop—This point is on the Small Intestine Meridian, located on the little finger side of each hand. This point is often associated with sadness and for the correction of psychological reversals (internal conflict).

Side of Thumb—This point is on the Lung Meridian, located on the side of the thumbnail of each hand, away from the other fingers. This point is often associated with sadness, grief, and intolerance.

Back of Hand (Gamut point)—This point is on the Triple Warmer Meridian, located on the back of the hand, between the little-finger and ring-finger knuckles. This point is often used in a bridging technique called the Nine-Gamut procedure (see description below) to enhance the results and balance the brain. It is also helpful for managing stress, physical pain, and depression.

The Nine-Gamut Procedure

Tap on the Gamut point (back of the hand between the little-finger and ring-finger knuckles) while doing these nine different actions.

1. Close Eyes

2. Open Eyes

3. Keeping your head still—look sharply down to your right side

4. Keeping your head still—look sharply down to your left side

5. Roll your eyes clockwise

6. Roll your eyes counter clockwise

7. Hum a tune for a few seconds

8. Count 1,2,3,4 or 2, 4, 6, etc.

9. Hum a tune for a few seconds.

Now come to center with your eyes. Take a few deep breaths and reevaluate your SUDS level. If there is any remaining distress present, do the following:

- Repeat your affirmation and include "still" and "some." For example, "Even though I **still** have **some** (state issue/problem), I deeply love and accept myself." and rub the Sore Spots or tap on the Karate Chop point while repeating the above affirmation.

- Next repeat the Primary Acupoint sequence tapping.
- This may take several rounds, so repeat as necessary.

Remember to use the information you have gathered to create the storyline you want to recover from. Obviously, this does not erase the event or memory. However, this exercise can help to release any traumatic or incapacitating energy involved with the memory. You will more than likely have more than one aspect of an issue, so be patient and know that you are whittling away at the issue one aspect at a time. Often, if the issue is the loss of a loved one, the SUDS level may only go down to a two (zero means no distress, and ten means the most stress one can imagine). This is understandable because there will most likely never be a time when you do not miss your loved one. However, being able to remember him or her without the incapacitating pain of doing so is the goal, not the absence of sadness over the loss.

Now let us review the steps once again:

1. Determine your SUDS level.

2. Create an affirmation using this model:

   "Even though I have this (issue or problem), I deeply love and accept myself, even this part of me."

3. Rub the Sore Spots or tap on the Karate Chop points while repeating your affirmation three times aloud.

4. Create a reminder phrase.

5. Tap seven-to-ten times on each point while repeating the reminder phase. Do this for three rounds.

6. Do the Nine-Gamut procedure.

7. Reassess your SUDS level.

8. Repeat, if necessary, adding the words "still" and "some" to your affirmation.

You can use this technique on any issue or problem you want to work on; it has been shown to be very effective on relieving trauma and anxiety. Please refer to the appendix for an example of a few tapping scripts that may help you get started with this exercise. However, keep in mind the more personalized the wording, the better the results will be. For more information on the research involved with this technique, please refer to the Recommended Reading and References section of this book.

Chapter 8:
Transforming the Inner Critic

We must rid ourselves of yesterday's negative thoughts to receive today's new positive feelings.

--Sydney Banks

We cannot change anything unless we accept it. Condemnation does not liberate; it oppresses.

--Carl Jung

You don't have to listen to any voice that does not bring you peace.

--Unknown Author

Our moods or emotions reflect the thoughts (conscious and subconscious) that create our lives. In the popular movie and book, *The Secret,* by Rhonda Byrne, part of this process is described; however, both the movie and the book neglect to mention that subconscious blocks often conflict with one's deepest desires. The key to actually using the mind to consciously create (bring into matter) one's desires is to unlock repressed emotions, memories, or sabotaging beliefs, and then transform this energy while accessing both the subconscious and conscious mind. The following techniques are designed to integrate awareness between both the conscious and subconscious mind. Thus, by healing internal conflict, one can release the emotional blockages that may exist within the mind and/or body.

The following meditations will assist you in connecting with your inner critic—the part of you that can sabotage your healing with internal conflict and self-criticism. Please remember to give yourself plenty of time and privacy to do these meditations. I have created an MP3 download titled *A Meditation to Transform Your Inner Critic* of these meditations. Visit my author page @ http://www.ozarkmt.com/ and receive your free download with the purchase of this book. Just use the code "Transform."

Meditation: Connecting to Your Inner Critic

Find a comfortable position and relax. Take a deep breath and hold... As you release, feel yourself relaxing and releasing any anxiety, tension, or worries you may have....

Take in another deep cleansing breath and hold... As you release, feel your muscles relaxing and releasing with each exhale....

Now take in one more deep cleansing breath and hold.... As you release, feel this wave of relaxation move down your body....

Now, as I count from 10 to 1, imagine yourself going deeper and deeper into your subconscious mind... toward a very special, safe, and comfortable place... this can be a memory or a fantasy—10, 9, 8, 7, 6, 5, 4, 3, 2, 1....

Now see yourself in this special place... you may see images, hear sounds in this environment, smell the aromas in the air, or feel the different textures on your skin... Remember, this is your special place, and it can be anything you wish for it to be....

Now call on your spiritual connection to be with you here in this special place... Feel the love, support, and wisdom your spiritual connection wants to share with you today.

Now imagine seeing a path opening up to you in this special place... It beckons to you... and with your spiritual connection by your side, you begin your journey moving forward on this path with courage and the inner knowing that this path will lead you to that critical part of you.

As you move along this path, notice each stepping stone or stumbling block you may encounter... Allow your spiritual connection to assist you in navigating around any blocks and celebrate each stepping stone along the way.

Now see yourself slowly approaching a beautiful crystal clear pond... As you slowly approach this pond, imagine yourself leaning over to drink from it... and notice your reflection in it...Take a moment to gaze upon this reflection of you...and now as if you are watching a movie, notice the form it takes as it begins to morph into that critical part of you... All the while, know that your spiritual connection is here supporting you.... Now allow this part of you to communicate with you.....Just allow this part of you to be heard...Avoid judging this information as you listen; hear the messages but avoid believing them... Just listen.... What message does this part of you want you to hear...?

Now ask how this part of you came to be...? What is its purpose...? Just listen.... Now let a name come to you that represents this part of you.... The first name that comes to you is the appropriate name for you to work with. ...Good. Now gather all the information you received and place it somewhere safe so you can bring it back with you... and slowly move away from the pond...and begin your journey back to the path that brought you here... Notice once again any stumbling blocks or stepping stones in the path leading you back, back to your special place.... Now take a moment to reflect upon your journey and the information you received....

Good. Now thank your spiritual connection for the guidance and support you received and slowly begin your journey back to this time and place as I count from 1 to 10—1, 2, 3, 4— bringing all the information you received back with you—5, 6, 7, 8, 9, 10.... All the way back now to this time and place....

Now become more aware of the room you're in... the time and place you're experiencing... take a deep breath, open your eyes, and—return to the room wide awake.

Journal Activity

Now just take a minute to write down your experience with an awareness of the story your inner critic shared with you.

Now go back to Chapter 7 and use the information you have gathered from your meditation. Using the same format, you can tap on the negative story or thoughts your inner critic shared with you until your SUDS level continues to decrease. When you have lowered your SUDS level to at least a two or three, return to the meditation below to continue your healing process.

Meditation: Transforming Your Inner Critic into Your Inner Guide

Find a comfortable position and relax. Take a deep breath and hold... as you release, feel yourself relaxing and releasing any anxiety, tension, or worries you may have....

Take in another deep cleansing breath and hold... as you release, feel your muscles relaxing and releasing with each exhale....

Now take in one more deep cleansing breath and hold.... As you release, feel this wave of relaxation move down your body....

Now count from 10 to 1; imagine yourself going deeper and deeper into your subconscious mind... towards a very special, safe, and comfortable place... This can be a memory or a fantasy—10, 9, 8, 7, 6, 5, 4, 3, 2, 1....

Now see yourself in this special place... You may see images, hear sounds in this environment, smell the aromas in the air, or feel the different textures on your skin... remember, this is your special place, and it can be anything you wish for it to be....

Now call on your spiritual connection to be with you here in this special place... Feel the love, support, and wisdom your spiritual connection wants to share with you today.

Now imagine seeing a path opening up to you in this special place... It beckons to you... and, with your spiritual connection by your side, you begin your journey moving forward on this path with an awareness and inner knowing that this path will lead you to an amazing discovery.

As you move along this path, notice each stepping stone, or if any stumbling blocks remain... allow your spiritual connection to assist you in navigating around any blocks and celebrate each stepping stone along the way.

Now see yourself slowly approaching a beautiful crystal clear pond... As you slowly approach this pond, imagine yourself leaning over to drink from it... and notice your reflection in it...Take a moment to gaze upon this reflection of you...and notice the form that reflects back to you.... Notice the changes that have occurred after releasing the erroneous beliefs and negative energy that have accumulated throughout the years....

Notice the beautiful guide/Goddess that has been here awaiting your arrival...Just take a moment to reconnect to this part of you.... Listen to any messages s/he may have for you.... What name would this part of you like to be called...?

Now thank this part of you and see yourself slowly immersing yourself into the water of this pond... Feel this connection growing stronger as you allow yourself to open up and receive this Divine guidance, transforming your inner critic with an inner guide/Goddess that will guide you along this journey called life....

Now slowly emerge from the pond anew... and begin your journey back to the path that brought you here.... Notice on your journey back a clear pathway awaits you... as all of your stumbling blocks have been removed.... Notice feeling lighter as you approach your special place once again....

Good. Now thank your spiritual connection for the guidance and support you received and slowly begin your journey back to this time and place as I count from 1 to 10—1, 2, 3, 4—bringing all the information you received back with you—5, 6, 7, 8, 9, 10.... All the way back now to this time and this place....

Now become more aware of the room you're in... the time and place you're experiencing... Take a deep breath, open your eyes, and return to the room wide awake.

Journal Activity

Now take just a minute to write down your experience in your journal.

You may need to do this exercise several times, each time addressing another aspect of an issue you need to release to complete your healing journey. As you release the debilitating story from your inner critic, you gain power to create a new, much healthier story.

Remember to also include the information you have been journaling and gathering throughout this book to assist you in identifying any internal conflict you may need to work on. You can use this imagery exercise and the tapping together or separately.

I recommend that you continue to make notes in your journal of anything you experience as a result of using any of the various techniques mentioned in this book. You can use the information gathered with each technique presented in this section of the book. You may find that one technique works better than another, depending on the issue you are working on. Next we will work with the subtle energies of the body.

Chapter 9:
Working with Your Subtle Energy Bodies:
The Chakras and the Biofield (Aura)

Just because we cannot detect, perceive, or measure forces that Chinese doctors say are important in managing illness does not automatically mean that they do not exist.

--Andrew Weil, M.D.

There can be no transforming of darkness into light and apathy into movement without emotion.

--Carl Gustav Jung

First, I want to remind you that I covered a brief explanation of the body's energetic system in Chapter 5. However, as a reminder, the biofield (aura) is an electromagnetic field that surrounds the entire body. The biofield (see Figures 5.1 and 5.2) contains a person's energy, protects against harmful environmental energies, and helps us to connect with others. This field is affected by changes in our emotions and physical states. It acts as a filter for life energies.

The chakras are involved in transmuting higher vibrational energy into a usable form. This energy is then utilized by the body's endocrine and nervous systems. The chakras resemble whirling vortices of subtle energy. When the chakra is open or operating correctly, each vortex rotates clockwise. In this section, I present some additional techniques to assist you in releasing any blocks from your chakras and biofield. Please keep in mind the meditation "Release and Transform Burden...," as well as the Heart Massage presented in Chapter 6, also work on the biofield and chakras of the body.

The following exercises from Donna Eden work on Neurological Disorganization (when certain electromagnetic energies that affect the brain's function are out of balance) and on Systemic Energetic Interference (an imbalance within some part of the individual's energetic system). I recommend doing these exercises at least once a day. This can actually become part of a healing ritual, which I will cover in the next chapter. These exercises can improve the outcome of all the techniques covered in Part 3 of this book. Therefore, I recommend doing these in conjunction with all the techniques shared in Part 3, as well as any other healing techniques you may be using on your own. This is based on Donna Eden's Daily Energy Routine and has been reprinted with permission by Innersource. For more information on these and many other wonderful healing techniques, please visit www.LearnEnergyMedicine.com.

Donna Eden's Five Minute Daily Routine
(Based on Donna Eden's Daily Energy Routine)

The Hook Up: Centers Energy

• Place the middle finger of one hand just above the nose.

• Place the middle finger of the other hand in the belly button

• Hold and pull up slightly for about 1-3 minutes

• Switch hands & repeat.

Three Thumps: Increases Energy & Strengthens Immune System

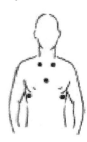

• With fingertips and thumb, massage/tap points shown in picture.

• Breathe deeply at each point.

Cross Crawl: Balances Energies & Clears Thinking

• March in place in this way:

• Lift right arm & left leg simultaneously.

• Next lift left arm & right leg.

• Repeat at least 12 to 20 times.

Figure Eights: Strengthens & Crosses Energy

- Make figure 8 patterns in front & on sides with both hands & arms.

- Use a swinging motion making small and/or large figure 8 patterns.

Wayne Cook Posture: Unscrambles Energy, Calms, & Clears Thinking

- Sit on edge of chair & place ankle on top of left knee.

- Place left hand on top of ankle.

- Wrap right hand around ball of the foot—take 5-7 deep breaths.

- Repeat same posture for other side.

- Uncross legs, place thumb & finger tips together and place above bridge of nose.

- Take 2 deep breaths.

Crown Pull: Clears the Mind & Calms Nervous System

- Bring both hands to forehead, placing fingertips on center of forehead just above eyebrows.

• With gentle pressure, pull fingers apart toward hairline

• Repeat this all the way to back of head & down to bottom of hairline.

• Next place hands on shoulders & gently pull forward, letting hands fall.

Separating Heaven & Earth: Creates Space in Joints

• Stand with hands on thighs, fingers spread, & take a deep breath.

• Bring your arms up above your head and then into prayer position.

• Inhale through your nose. Stretch one arm up & one down.

• Pushing with your palms, turn head/neck facing the side of the raised arm—hold 5+ seconds.

• Switch sides and repeat 5 times.

• Drop arms down and bend forward at the waist.

• Relax with knees slightly bent.

• Take a few deep breaths (also you can do figure 8s if you wish) and slowly return to standing position.

Zip Up: Increases Confidence, Self-Protection, & Clears Thinking

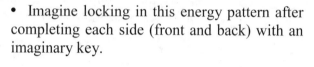

- Rub hands together & shake off.

- Using hands or fingertips, trace from the top of your pubic bone to lower lip 2-3 times.

- Now trace from the tail bone over the head to your upper lip 2-3 times.

- Imagine locking in this energy pattern after completing each side (front and back) with an imaginary key.

Now that we have your energies balanced, we are going to work on the individual chakras, but first let me briefly review a bit of information on them. The crown (7th) chakra is at the crown/top of the head and is usually represented by the color white. The brow (6th) chakra, located just above the middle of the eyebrows and sometimes referred to as the third eye, is often represented by the color violet. The throat (5th) chakra, located mid-throat, is represented by the color blue. The heart (4th) chakra, located mid-chest, is usually represented by the color green. The solar plexus (3rd) chakra, located in the middle of the upper stomach region, is represented by the color yellow. The sacral (2nd) chakra, located in the mid-abdominal are, is represented the color orange, and lastly, the root (1st) chakra, located at the tailbone or the end of the spine, is represented by the color red. You can refer back to Chapter 5 for a visual representation of the chakras if this helps you to visualize them.

The Chakra Cleanse

Root Chakra: Find a comfortable position and bring your awareness into your body. Perhaps take a few deep breaths to help you center. Now we will begin with the root (1st) chakra located at the tailbone. Focus your attention on your root chakra; let yourself become aware of any emotions you may experience here, especially around survival and safety issues. With the palm of your right hand towards your body in front of the root chakra, begin moving your right hand in a counter-clockwise motion (towards the thumb)—this cleans the chakra. Allow any negative emotions that may come up to be released. When this feels complete, take a deep cleansing breath and begin moving your right hand in a clockwise motion (towards your little finger) and visualize the color red—this balances and locks in the new energetic pattern.

Sacral Chakra: Next move your right hand to your sacral (2nd) chakra located in your mid-abdominal area. Focus your attention on your sacral chakra; let yourself be aware of any emotions, especially around choosing, manifesting, and sexuality. With the palm of your right hand towards your body, begin moving your right hand in a counter-clockwise (towards your thumb) motion. Allow any negative emotions that may come up to be released. When this feels complete, take a deep cleansing breath, begin moving your right hand in a clockwise motion (towards your little finger), and visualize the color orange to balance this chakra.

Solar Plexus Chakra: Next continue working your way up the body and move your right hand to the solar plexus (3rd) chakra located on the upper stomach region. Allow yourself to be aware of any emotions, especially around lack of self-esteem and/or feelings of powerlessness. With the palm of your right hand towards your body, begin moving your right hand in a counter-clockwise (toward your thumb) motion. Allow any negative emotions that may come up to be released. When this feels complete, take a deep cleansing breath, begin moving your right hand in a clockwise (towards your little finger) motion, and visualize the color yellow to balance this chakra.

Heart Chakra: Next continue to your heart (4th) chakra, located mid-chest. With the palm of your right hand towards your body, begin moving your right hand in a counter-clockwise (towards your thumb) motion over your heart chakra. Allow any negative emotions that may come up to be released, especially those involving forgiveness of self or another and feelings of an inability to love. When this feels complete, take a deep cleansing breath, begin moving your right hand in a clockwise (towards the little finger) motion, and visualize the color green to balance this chakra.

Throat Chakra: Next continue to your throat (5th) chakra located mid-throat. With the palm of your right hand towards your body, begin moving your right hand in a counter-clockwise (towards thumb) motion over your throat chakra. Allow any negative emotions that may come up to be released, especially around an inability to express yourself or any feelings of being unheard. When this feels complete, take a deep cleansing breath, begin moving your right hand in a clockwise (towards your little finger) motion, and visualize the color blue to balance this chakra.

Brow Chakra: Next continue to your brow (6th) chakra, often referred to as the "third eye," located mid-forehead just above the eyebrows. With the palm of your right hand towards your body, begin moving your right hand in a counter-clockwise (towards thumb) motion over your Brow chakra. Allow any negative emotions that may come up to be released, especially around fear and an inability to see clearly. When this feels complete, take a deep cleansing breath, begin moving your right hand in a clockwise (towards little finger) motion, and visualize the color violet or indigo to balance this chakra.

Crown Chakra: Next continue to your crown (7th) chakra located at the top (crown) of your head. With the palm of your right hand towards your body, begin moving your right hand in a counter-clockwise (towards thumb) motion over your crown chakra. Note, many practices advise moving the right hand in the opposite direction from the other chakras over the crown. I have found the intention of the individual is what is most important here. However, please use whatever technique feels more comfortable to you. Now allow any negative emotions that may come up to be released, especially around feelings of anger at and any disconnection from your spiritual connection. When this feels complete, take a deep cleansing breath, begin moving your right hand in a clockwise (towards little finger) motion, and visualize the color white to balance this chakra.

Zip-Up: Now, refer to the Zip-Up technique in Donna Eden's 5 minute routine presented earlier in this chapter and use this technique to "Zip-Up" your energy field.

Journal Activity

I encourage you to take a few minutes to process any information that you may have become aware of during this exercise and write it down in your journal.

Remember that you can use this information with the other techniques presented in this section of the book. Next we will work with the biofield or aura.

Please refer to Chapter 5 for a visual representation (Figures 5.1 and 5.2) and review of the biofield. The following exercise will assist you in clearing and strengthening your biofield. Remember: the Release and Transform Burden Meditation mentioned in Chapter 6 can also assist you with this process.

The Brush-Down Exercise

In this exercise, bring your awareness to an event that was upsetting to you. Perhaps, think of a loss that has occurred or your response to it.

Now while sitting or standing, take a few deep breaths and set your intention to let go of any negative effects that this event has had on you.

With your next inhalation, bring the palms of your hands, facing outward, above your head. As you exhale, let your hands "brush down" your biofield—head-to-toe, side-to-side, and imagine doing this behind you as well. Allow yourself to sigh or groan loudly as you exhale.

Now continue this process on your body—brushing your arms, under your arms, the upper and lower torso, the groin area, legs, and feet.

Remember to keep your intention to release in mind as you do this exercise and use your breath to assist you in letting go of any negative emotion you may experience.

Now when this feels complete, bring your hands together in a prayer position and bring a color to mind, the first color that comes to mind is the appropriate one for you to work with.

Next imagine this color filling your entire biofield, sealing any rips, tears, and/or releasing any remaining negative energy.

Journal Activity

Note any sensations you experience as you do this exercise and write these in your journal. This information may be used with other techniques shared in this book, as well as assisting in your healing journey.

Now that we have worked with our subtle energy, chakras and Biofield, we will turn to another powerful recovery tool that indigenous cultures have used for centuries—ritual.

Chapter 10:
Healing Rituals:
Releasing, Remembering,
Redefining, and Rediscovering

*Rituals give significance to life's passages. They provide form
and guidance to our lives, prescribing behaviors during
perilous times when bodies, minds, and spirits are broken.
Without rituals, we would have no map for how to act, no
occasions for people to share their common bonds and
experiences.*

--Achterberg, Dossey, & Kolkmeier
Rituals of Healing: Using Imagery for Health and Wellness

Healing rituals have been used for centuries. However, I
believe that Western culture lacks an appreciation and
understanding of the power of ritual. Although ritual can be
found in many churches and other organizations, the meaning
behind these rituals is often misunderstood or is missing
altogether. Nevertheless, I do want to acknowledge those
rituals that address the loss of a loved one, such as a memorial
or funeral. Unfortunately, for many losses, there are no such
rituals in place. In addition, once the memorial or funeral is
complete, often there are no other ceremonies wherein one can
continue to process and release all of the emotions that
continue to emerge as time moves forward. Therefore, I
encourage and assist others in creating their own healing rituals
that fit into their own unique belief systems.

Rituals can reduce anxiety and feelings of helplessness. Rituals
can invite family and community support, as well as encourage
self-acceptance and compassion. Most importantly, rituals

often produce a sense of spiritual connection and tap into a higher sense of self.

For any ritual to work best, we must understand the meaning behind the acts and believe in their significance. First, let us define ritual and explore the elements/components of a ritual. Here are a few dictionary definitions: *an established and prescribed pattern of observance, e.g., in a religion; the observance of actions or procedures in a set, ordered, and ceremonial way; a pattern of actions or words followed regularly and precisely* (online Encarta Dictionary, English North American version) and so forth.

What is missing from these definitions is the most important element: intention. Lynne McTaggart wrote about the power of intention in her book *The Intention Experiment: Using Your Thoughts to Change Your Life and the World.* Whether one's intention is to release, remember, rediscover, or create healing in some way—without attention to the intention, the ritual behavior just becomes a routine. McTaggart's research also suggests that the power of intention multiplies, depending on the number of people holding the same intent. Therefore, I encourage you to come together with other like-minded individuals to multiply your results.

The rituals I present in this chapter are examples of what I have used personally and professionally to assist in releasing the energy of grief. These rituals invite you to go deep within to express what may have been repressed. Once again, I invite you to use the information you have uncovered as a result of the other exercises you have used in this book. Go back to your journal, and as you browse through it, notice any themes around your losses. Use this information to assist with releasing, remembering, redefining, and rediscovering yourself.

Releasing Rituals

Burning/Burying Ceremony

The following ritual can be performed in a group or individually. First, take your time and write down on a separate piece of paper what it is you want to release—an emotion, a negative belief, and so on. Take some time to reflect upon your loss and let any additional feelings or thoughts you may have come into your awareness. Perhaps you can use the information you have been gathering throughout this book. However, please be sure to use a separate piece of paper that is safe to burn or bury.

Now after you have written down what you are ready to release, gather this information and create a "burning ceremony." This can be accomplished many ways, from simple to elaborate. For example, if done in a group format, each member can say a few words before releasing his or her paper into a campfire or fire pit while others chant or simply remain silent. If you are doing this ceremony alone, you can simply burn your paper in a fireproof container. Whichever way you perform this ritual, your intention is to release what no longer serves you. See the ashes going to the heavens or perhaps imagine a phoenix rising from the ashes.

Another variation of this ritual is a "burial ceremony." This is done by burying your list in a significant location. Often a flower, tree, or something that has significance can also be planted where you bury your list, or you may choose to combine a few variations. The most important thing is to remember your intention.

Now allow yourself some time to process your emotions. Write your experience(s) in your journal for exploring further, perhaps with some of the other healing techniques shared in this book.

Chanting

There are many forms of chanting. I recommend getting a CD of your favorite chants or refer to the Recommended Readings and References section of this book for some of my favorite artists. If you prefer, there may be a group or church near you that offers chanting. This technique can also be combined with other techniques, especially when done in a group format. For example, the group may chant while you release your list of concerns in a burning/burial ceremony. First, whether you are in a group or choose to do this alone, set your intention to release. As you chant, let you feelings rise to the surface to be released through your vocal cords. Allow these vibrations to permeate every cell of your body. Use your breath as well to assist you in releasing any negative or painful emotions.

The God Box

This is also a releasing ritual. When referring to this box, please use whatever name feels most comfortable to you—God/Goddess, Higher Power, Source, etc. This ritual can be performed in a group or individually. Initially, you will want to allow yourself or the group a significant amount of time to create your God box.

First, find a small box about the size of a tissue box with a lid. Depending on the box, you might want to cut an opening in the top of the box. Now, decorate it with something significant. You can cut out pictures from magazines, use old photos, draw symbols, etc. This box represents your "God/Goddess," so be creative and know that this is also part of the healing process. If this is performed in a group, each person can decorate his or her own box, or the group can decorate a bigger box. Note, this box will be used again and again, so plan accordingly.

After the "God Box" has been created, take some time to write down on a sheet of paper or index card what you would like to let go of—worries, emotions, thoughts, anything you are ready to release. Perhaps it would be helpful to once again refer back to your journal to assist you with this process.

When I do this exercise in a group, I often do a brief guided meditation that also assists with this process. Therefore, I invite you to play some music and let yourself go deep into meditation with the intention of gathering up what no longer serves you and visualize yourself "letting go and letting God."

Then place your list inside your God box, and any time you catch yourself thinking about any of the issues you have placed in this box, I want you to imagine or literally go to your God box and say something like: "Thank you, God. I want this issue back. I think I can do a much better job of resolving it than you." This is a powerful reminder that will assist you in your continual efforts to release all that no longer serves you.

I often combine this ritual with the Heart Massage technique (see Figure 6.1) mentioned in Chapter 6. Simply do the Heart Massage techniques while placing your list in your God box and repeat the following statement: "Even though I've held onto this/these issue(s), I'm willing to let go of it/them now. I'm willing to open my heart and receive love once again. I'm willing to release this/these burden(s). I'm willing to forgive and be forgiven."

Balloon Release

This is a simple exercise that has tremendous power for children and adults. It can also be used as a Remembering Ritual (see the Remembering Section). Once again, it is your intention that will determine how you proceed with this exercise. To use it as a release ritual, write down on small pieces of biodegradable paper (you may also write on the balloons themselves) everything you want to release—feelings, thoughts, etc.

Now tie these pieces of paper to biodegradable balloons filled with helium. (Latex is a naturally occurring material made from tree sap and is biodegradable).

Next determine if there is a special place where you would like to release your balloons, such as the cemetery, park, backyard, and so forth.

Now with your intention to release what you have written, let go of your balloon(s). You might imagine the balloon(s) going to Source, God, or Heaven; whatever feels most appropriate to you. This is often done on an anniversary or some other significant milestone as a way to release any challenging emotions related to the loss.

Breath-Work for Releasing

There are several forms of breath-work for healing. What I am presenting here is a form of progressive relaxation and breath-work for releasing subconscious body memories at a cellular level. Please keep in mind that your intention and your willingness to release is all that is required with this ritual. As with the other previously mentioned rituals, this one can be done individually or with a group. Your intention here is to release all that no longer serves you with each exhale.

First, find a place where you can lie down or sit in a comfortable position.

Now, take a deep breath in and hold it while simultaneously tensing your scalp muscles as tight as you can and hold for just a few seconds (10-15 seconds).

When you release, exhale completely and forcefully.

Now continuing down your body, take another deep breath in and tighten you facial muscles. Hold for a few seconds, and once again, when you release, exhale completely and forcefully.

Next move to your neck and shoulders. Tighten them and take in a deep breath and hold. Now release, exhaling completely and forcefully.

Do the same thing with your arms and fists. Tighten as you take in a deep breath and release, exhaling completely and forcefully.

Now move to your stomach and abdominal muscles. Tighten as you take in a deep breath and release, exhaling completely and forcefully.

Move to your hips and buttocks. Tighten as you take in a deep breath and release, exhaling completely and forcefully.

Now move to your legs and feet. Tighten as you take in a deep breath and release, exhaling completely and forcefully.

Finally, tighten all your muscles as you take in a deep breath, releasing anything remaining with a forceful exhale.

As you do this exercise, please remember to set your intention to release any subconscious body memories related to your loss. I recommend doing this release at least once daily, perhaps before you go to sleep or whenever it best fits into your schedule.

Story Telling With EFT

Story telling has been used by indigenous cultures for centuries and always has a way of healing. However, when combined with the Emotional Freedom Technique (EFT), it can be an even more powerful way of releasing pain at a cellular level. As with the other rituals, this can be done alone or with a group. However, keep in mind the impact of group energy, and if possible, find an appropriate group to share this ritual with.

If this ritual is done in a group format, everyone in the group should tap along with each member's story. Remember to set the intention to release the emotional pain attached to your story. For example, if you are telling the story about the loss of a loved one, such as in a bereavement group, everyone would simply tap along using the EFT format shared in Chapter 7. However, do not be concerned about setting up an affirmation or determining your SUDS level at this time, just tap on the points while sharing your story. Then move on to the next group member. If doing this exercise alone, just repeat your story aloud while tapping on the various acupoints (see Figure 7.1) until you have completed your entire story. As always, notice your experience and journal any awareness or insights you may have.

Another technique to assist with releasing is the "Release & Transform Burden" meditation in Chapter 6. For maximum benefit, I recommend listening to the CD, which is available on my website: www.mindbodyspirit-innergrations.com. These are just a few Releasing rituals to get you started. You can combine these rituals or modify them to fit your needs. Next we will explore Remembering Rituals.

Remembering Rituals

These rituals are often used to assist with remembering a loved one. I am including a pet in this category. This commemorates the loved one and assists the bereaved to emotionally relocate his or her loved one from the outside to the inside of themselves. Often individuals are afraid to move forward for fear they will forget or dishonor their loved ones if they recover from their loss. These rituals help to keep memories alive and allow for release of the fear of moving forward. These rituals are often performed on anniversaries or significant milestones within a person's life. However, they can be done at any time to assist us in our recovery process. As with all the other rituals previously mentioned, our intentions are important. These rituals can be done with a group or individually.

The Memory Box

This is a very simple yet powerful ritual. I have actually found pre-made boxes for this ritual; however, you may want to create your own. Your intention here is to gather items of significance that will trigger positive memories of your loved one. You may want to do this ritual as a family, individually, or both. I encourage you to set aside a specific amount of time, play some music that is also significant and build you memories with intention. Remember your intent is to honor your loved one, as well as address any fears of forgetting him or her. Place all the items you have gathered in your "memory box" and put it somewhere special for safekeeping. You may want to create an altar to place your memory box on. This altar can include whatever feels significant for you—religious figures, keepsakes, etc. Know that you can continue to update your memory box and altar as you continue to recover from your loss.

Balloon Release

We used this is in the release ritual section, but it can also be used here as a Remembering Ritual. Your intention will be to connect with that which you have lost. You may want to write down on small pieces of biodegradable paper (or directly onto the balloons) everything you want to remember—feelings, thoughts, etc. Now tie these pieces of paper to biodegradable balloons filled with helium. (Latex is a naturally occurring material made from tree sap and is biodegradable).

Next determine if there is a special place where you would like to release your balloons, such as the cemetery, park, backyard, and so forth.

Now with your intention to remember what you have written, release your balloon(s). You might imagine the balloon(s) going to Source, God, or Heaven, whichever feels most appropriate to you.

This is often done on an anniversary or some other significant milestone to remember what you have lost. Most often, this is done in memory of a loved one with the intention to connect.

Light a Candle Ritual

There are many variations of this ritual, and I encourage you to make it your own. I have done this ritual in various forms with my family and my bereavement group. It can be performed for any occasion where you want to remember your loved one. Again, it is the intent and meaning behind this ritual that supports the healing that transpires.

First, I recommend using a long burning candle that has a container around it.

The following is a poem that I found helpful to include with this ritual. I encourage you to read it only if it resonates with you. If done in a group, you may want to designate a person to read the poem or light the candle.

Remember to personalize this ritual with your own unique actions. Now if you choose to, read the following poem as you light your candle or simply say what is in your heart.

Light a candle;

See it glow.

Watch it dance when you feel low.

Think of our light; we will always be here day or night.

A candle flickers out of sight,

But in your heart, we still burn bright.

Think not of sadness, that we are not near.

Think of gladness & joyous cheer.

We have not left you: we are not gone.

We are here to stay, my little one.

So when you light a candle & see it glow, watch it dance,

And in your heart you will know that we have never left you.

Even when you have felt so blue,

Know that we are sitting up here with the Lord

& now we are watching over you.

--Unknown Author--

You can modify this ritual to meet your needs. For example, in the above poem, you can replace the "We" with "I" if you are doing this in the memory of an individual loved one. You can light a candle without saying or reading a poem, with the intention of remembering your loved one any time you want. In my bereavement group, we light a candle at the beginning of the group gathering, commemorating each individual who has died. Then at the close of the gathering, we blow out the candle, "taking their light with us." Please use this ritual in whatever way is most helpful to you.

The Butterfly Ritual

This ritual, like many of the other rituals, can also be used as a releasing ritual. However, for now, I am placing it under the category of a Remembering Ritual. You can obtain butterflies for this ritual simply by going online and using the keywords: "butterflies for butterfly release." You will get several sites listed, and at this point, I do not have enough information on any of these sites to recommend one over another. You may also decide to obtain your own butterflies and make them part of the ritual—finding, catching, and releasing them.

First, I would like to share a story about the significance of this ritual for me and how I found it helpful. Every year, the Cancer Support Community of Central Indiana has an event called the Survivors Symposium. At this event, participants have a butterfly release in memory of those who have died from cancer.

The year after my nephew, Shane, died from cancer, I released a butterfly in his memory. We were each given a small envelope containing a butterfly. Upon opening the envelope, the butterfly is somewhat disoriented and dormant. It takes a few minutes for the butterfly to wake up and begin flapping its wings. Waiting for my butterfly to begin this process allowed me ample time to see what type (color) I had.

Now I did not really give this part of the process much thought at the time; however, it became very significant to me much later as I began writing this book. It was in Chapter One when I was sharing my nephew's story that I began having a very difficult time emotionally. Therefore, I sat outside on my patio to write because it is one of my healing sanctuaries. The patio is about seventeen feet off the ground and is surrounded by trees, so it is like my own private tree house. I am continuously surrounded by the sounds of various songbirds, and connecting with nature has always helped me to gain clarity; however, this day was even more special.

Although it is common for me to see birds and squirrels, I cannot remember a time before or since that I actually saw butterflies so high up in the trees. As I began writing and remembering the journey I had taken with my sister and nephew, the tears flowed. These tears became paralyzing, and I had to stop writing.

Suddenly as I sat there in my grief, a butterfly began dancing in the air in front of me. It slowly came to a halt right on the page I was writing on—this was the exact same kind of butterfly I had released several months earlier in my nephew's honor. It stayed awhile and seemed to speak to me, letting me know that Shane had simply transitioned, and it was a gentle reminder—letting me know the importance of completing this book. Then, all of a sudden, another butterfly approached and danced once again in the air in front of me, encouraging the other butterfly to join in the fun and remind me that Shane was not alone. Then both butterflies flew away, playing and enjoying the beautiful day.

This healing moment has stayed with me and assisted me in profound ways. It allowed me to continue my writing, healing, and releasing my grief along the way. I encourage you to use this ritual in such a way that you may find a way to release, remember, and enjoy life once again.

Before you can begin this ritual, you must decide how you will obtain your butterflies. As I have suggested, you may order them online or include finding, catching, and releasing them as part of your own ritual. As with the other rituals, you can do this in a group or alone.

Once you have your butterflies, set aside some time and a place that has meaning for you—the time can perhaps be an anniversary, a birthday, or other significant time.

Before you release your butterfly, remember to connect with it and remember the significance of releasing it in memory of your loved one or what you have lost. Your intention is the most important part here; however, I encourage you to remember the symbolism of the butterfly as a form of transition.

Once again, you may wish to write down in your journal any significant thoughts or feelings you may have before, during, and after this ritual. You can also use this information along with some of the other techniques in this book to assist you to release and continue your healing process.

Journaling Ritual

Throughout this book I have suggested and encouraged you to record your experiences in your journal. Now I am suggesting that you use journaling as a form of ritual to connect with yourself, your loved one, or what you have lost. I have used this technique with my clients to assist them in remembering what was lost to reassure them that those memories will always exist. This is also a tremendous way to connect with a loved one. Below is an example of a short story that was written by a man who lost his wife. He and his wife had raised and rescued many dogs/cats prior to his wife's death. I have reprinted this story with his permission.

Reunion

--Mike Silver—

Rain continued to spill from the sky. The eight animals huddled together. The five dogs stand helplessly, their fur drenched and plastered to their skins. Three cats huddled under the bridge where they stayed dry. "We were always smarter than those dogs," they thought. They were right.

"Why are we here?" they wondered. "Some of us have met before, but who are the others?" Kelly, the larger black dog, stared curiously at the small orange Persian cat.

"I think he said his name was Barney," she said to herself.

They met just a few minutes ago. Kelly, the caretaker, had to know everyone's name, so she would know whom to help when asked.

The rain began to slow and came to a merciful end. Sunshine warmed the wet dogs and felt good to the cats, who slowly came out from under the bridge.

Cassie, ever the watchful one, saw the figure first and began her warning bark. Daisy, who had been here the longest, didn't even bother to look. She had seen this before. A human comes, looks around the bridge, then goes on its way.

Cody, the greyhound, began wagging his tail. But then, he did that whenever he saw a person. The others ignored him.

The person approached and suddenly Barney raised his tail, cried out and began running toward her. Kelly yipped and followed with Cassie in hot pursuit. The others held back.

"It can't be. It's way too early. That is not who we think it is. Why would she be here? Now?"

Yet here she was. In one way this was a joyous surprise. In another way, it was a total shock. She tearfully scooped up Barney and held him close. Cassie ran in circles round and round her. Cody leaned on her, waiting to be petted and admired.

She walked toward the multi-colored bridge to greet the others—passive Charlie, the small black dog; Daisy, the first pet; Tony and Abby, brother and sister who had just been reunited.

She could not pet them or kiss them enough. How she missed them all!

Slowly she rose to her feet with Barney and Charlie in her arms and the rest following close behind. Together they crossed the Rainbow Bridge with the most joyous feeling any of them had ever experienced.

As they walked down the other side of the bridge, Kelly, Cody, and Abby looked back, then up at her with questioning stares.

"He will come later," she said. "Much later, I hope. There are still things to do."

The sun began to set as the nine figures strolled happily away from the bridge, anticipating the day when they would come back for the final reunion.

Next is an example of a poem that was written by a woman who lost her husband.

Bringing Thoughts to Me

--Donna Pittman--

Sitting on a mother's lap a young child talked and talked,

Asking questions one by one as they rocked and rocked.

Turning, squirming, smiling, hugging...what a precious sight...

Bringing thoughts to me of Mother...Mother in the light.

Two children swinging in a swing, up in the air so high,

Singing the poem that Grandma sang while pushing my swing to the sky.

Reciting poems as we walked to the woods...a picnic by the trees...

Bringing thoughts to me of Grandma, Grandma in the breeze.

Riding on a tractor, plowing up the weeds...

Spreading manure, feeding the pigs, eating beach nuts from the trees.

Milking the cows, planting the wheat, picking all the corn...

Bringing thoughts to me of Grandpa...Grandpa in the morn'.

Hunting squirrels in the woods, listening to the wind...

Finding the stream, luring the fish...shu-u...fingers to lips...quiet.

Tracking deer in the cold winter snow, finding a cave for warmth...

Watching the sky for signs gone by...thoughts of Dad.

Daniel moved to San Diego...far, far, away...

Daniel tall, strong, and young...grown and gone away.

John died last November, turning 'round to the sun...

Riddled and shrunken with cancer...his journey on earth was done.

Now I'm alone in my sorrow, wondering how life passed me by.

Longing to be with my family, way up there in the sky.

The Next Day

--Donna Pittman--

Opening my soul to my sadness,

The breeze gently touches my face.

The sun warms me all over

While the streams trickle and race.

Oceans, deserts, mountains and fields,

Provide the awesome expanse,

And Nature in all her glory

Invites the infinite dance.

Blessed be!

These are just few examples of journaling as a form of ritual. Many of my clients have written poetry, as well as letters to those they have lost. The most important part of this ritual is your intent to connect with what you have lost. Just allow yourself to let words, symbols, colors, and so forth, come to you while you create from this space of reconnecting.

You can also draw or write. Perhaps playing some music that reminds you of what you have lost will assist you with this exercise. Avoid getting caught up in spelling, grammar, or any other errors. You will not be graded or judged on this exercise, nor do you have to share it with anyone.

Allow yourself ample time and space to do this ritual. You may want to do it daily, weekly, monthly, or whenever it feels right to you. Many have used this ritual as a way to share what they wish they had said to a loved one prior to death or some other form of separation. Please remember you can combine this with the tapping techniques to further assist you in your recovery process.

Redefining and Rediscovering Rituals

Let us not regret the past. Let us not worry about the future. Go back to the present moment and live deeply the present moment—because the present moment is the only moment where you can touch life. Life is available only in the present moment.

Thich Nhat Hanh
Resting in the River, Shambhala Sun

These rituals are a form of self-exploration. They are a catalyst for self-growth and an attempt to answer the following questions:

Who am I?

What can I do without?

How do I feel safe again?

How can I make myself feel better?

As with all the other rituals previously mentioned, this can be done with a group or individually. Please note your intention before proceeding with this or any of the rituals mentioned.

The Labyrinth

A labyrinth is a pattern with a purpose. It is not a maze where one can get lost or confused; rather, it is a chance to find order out of chaos. It offers a chance to take a "time out" from our busy stress-filled lives and find ourselves once again. Walking or tracing a labyrinth can lead to self-discovery, new insights, and a sense of balance, well-being and connectedness.

There is a deep human need to seek order out of chaos. The labyrinth can represent our passage through time and our many experiences in life. Its many turns reflect "the journey of life," which involves change and transition. Unlike a maze, which has dead ends, the labyrinth has a single path leading to the center.

As we enter the path, we are purposefully entering a space where there is order and reason. Walking or tracing a labyrinth gives us the opportunity to look deeply within ourselves as we follow a path to the very center of our being and connect once again to our higher selves. It can symbolize that no time or effort is ever wasted; if we stay the course, every step takes us closer to our goal of self-discovery.

Like life, walking or tracing a labyrinth is more about the journey rather than the destination, about *being* rather than *doing*. This process integrates body, mind, and soul. I invite you to experience this as a tool in your self-discovery process. I have included a labyrinth you can use (see Figure 10.1) for this exercise. However, walking a labyrinth can actually be even more powerful, and many churches and other organizations offer labyrinths that you can use. Regardless of whether you choose to walk your local labyrinth or utilize the one I have provided, the intention for self-discovery, reflection, and awareness remains the same.

Before you begin, make sure you have set aside time (approximately 30 minutes or more) and have your journal ready to write down your experience. If you are tracing the labyrinth provided, I recommend you make a copy, and if you desire, enlarge it. I use some sort of meditative music (for suggestions, see Recommended Readings and References) while doing this exercise. Walk or trace the labyrinth at your own pace but remember to allow time for reflection to maximize your experience. Enjoy!

Figure 10.1

Journal Activity

Now write down in your journal any insights or emotions you may have experienced. Remember, you can use this information with the other tools (i.e., inner critic meditation) in this book to assist you with your recovery and moving forward with your life.

Saturday Suppers

I had several ladies in one of my bereavement groups who had lost their husbands. During this time, they became very bonded. Helping each other with the loneliness from this loss became very important, and they decided to create what they called the "Saturday Suppers." These Saturday suppers are still going on after more than three years, and others (men and women) from my bereavement group have joined them. Unbeknownst to them, they had created a ritual of gathering for the purpose of rediscovering themselves without their spouses; I encourage you to join or start a group with the intention of rediscovering yourself apart from your loss.

Conclusion

In the following Appendix, you will find sample Tapping Scripts; however, I want to remind you of the importance of being as specific as possible with the statements you use with this exercise. Please remember that if you have any problems with this or any of the other techniques I have included in this book, contact a mental health care professional. I am also available for phone or individual sessions and can be reached on my website: www.mindbodyspirit-innergrations.com for more information.

Appendix A:
Sample Tapping Scripts

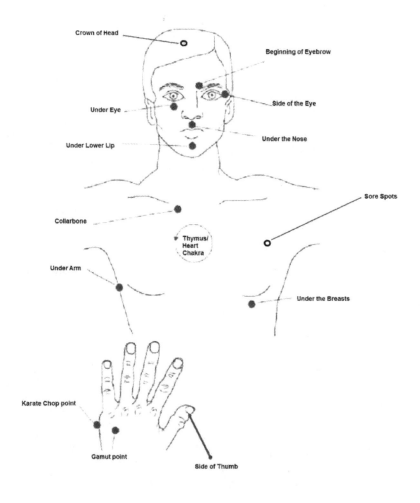

Appendix Figure 1

General Tapping Statements

Tune into your emotions, issue, or problem. Try to be as specific as possible. It may help to close your eyes and imagine the issue you want to work on as a movie:

- Who are the characters?

- What do you hear/see?

- What emotions and/or physical feelings are you experiencing?

Now rate this (SUDS level) in terms of how disturbing or stressful this feels: 0 = no distress/disturbance to 10 = highly stressful/disturbing.

Please be sure and write down this rating in your journal. You will need to refer back to this SUDS level to determine your progress.

Now tap on the Karate Chop or rub the Sore Spots (see Appendix Figure 1) and <u>say aloud three times</u> while tapping/rubbing:

"Even though a part of me has this issue (name the problem/issue), I deeply and completely accept this part of me."

You may also use the feeling state that you are experiencing:

"Even though a part of me feels (name the feeling/emotion), I deeply and completely accept this part of me."

Now tap between your eyebrows and say:

"I acknowledge and release any fear or trauma associated with this (issue/emotion) at its deepest level."

Tap on the side of the eye and say:

"I acknowledge and release any anger or rage associated with this (issue/emotion) at its deepest level."

Tap under both eyes and say:

"I acknowledge and I am willing to let go of any anxiety associated with this (issue/emotion) at its deepest level."

Tap under your nose and say:

"I acknowledge and release any blocks that would keep me from moving forward at the deepest level associated with this (issue/emotion)."

Tap under your lower lip and say:

"I acknowledge and release any shame or guilt associated with this (issue/emotion) at its deepest level."

Tap on the collarbone points and say:

"I acknowledge and release any feelings of numbness or shock at the deepest level associated with this (issue/emotion)."

Tap or do heart massage on the thymus/heart point and say:

"I acknowledge and release all sadness at its deepest level associated with this (issue/emotion) and I forgive myself.

Tap under your arms and say:

"I acknowledge and release any toxic beliefs and/or blocks to resolving this (issue/emotion) at its deepest level."

Tap under your breasts and say:

"I acknowledge and release any beliefs that cause me to be unhappy associated with this (issue/emotion) at its deepest level."

Tap the side of the thumb and say:

"I acknowledge and release any sense of grief or intolerance towards myself or another associated with this (issue/emotion) at its deepest level."

Now tap on the crown of your head and say:

"I acknowledge any anger, grief, or feelings of being punished by the Divine/God/Source, and I am willing to release this (issue/emotion) and know that I deserve peace."

Now rate your overall progress. Rate your SUDS level in terms of how disturbing or stressful the issue or emotion feels as you once again tune back into your "movie": 0 = no distress/disturbance and 10 = highly stressful/disturbing.

Be gentle with yourself and know that sometimes results are experienced rapidly; however, often, persistence may be required to tap away all aspects of an issue. Please contact a professional if your SUDS level goes up, or you experience any difficulty with this or any of the other exercises.

After completing three rounds of tapping on the negative issue/emotion, it may be helpful to complete the Nine-Gamut procedure mentioned earlier in Chapter 7.

Also, please refer to the end of this section for an example of Positive Tapping. Positive Tapping is usually completed after approximately three rounds of working on the negative issue/emotion, and/or after the Nine-Gamut procedure. The Positive Tapping technique is helpful in affirming what it is you want/choose to replace the negative emotion or issue with.

Tapping for Loss of a Relationship

Tune in to your emotions, issue, or problem. Try to be as specific as possible. It may be helpful to close your eyes and imagine the issue you want to work on as a movie:

- Who are the characters?

- What do you hear/see?

- What emotions and/or physical feelings are you experiencing?

Now rate this (SUDS level) in terms of how disturbing or stressful this feels: 0 = no distress/disturbance to 10 = highly stressful/disturbing.

Please be sure and write down this rating in your journal because you will need to refer back to this SUDS level to determine your progress.

Now tap on the Karate Chop or rub the Sore Spots (see Appendix Figure 1) and <u>say aloud three times</u> while tapping/rubbing:

> *"Even though a part of me feels (name the feeling/emotion), I deeply and completely accept this part of me."*

Now tap between your eyebrows and say:

> *"I acknowledge and release any fear or trauma associated with the loss of this relationship."*

Tap on the side of the eye and say:

> *"I acknowledge and release any anger or rage at myself or another."*

Tap under both eyes and say:

> *"I acknowledge and I am willing to let go of any anxiety associated with the loss of this relationship."*

Tap under your nose and say:

"I acknowledge and release any blocks that would keep me from moving forward towards a healthy relationship with myself or another."

Tap under your lower lip and say:

"I acknowledge and release any shame or guilt associated with the loss of this relationship."

Tap on the collarbone points and say:

"I acknowledge and release any feelings of numbness or shock at how this relationship ended."

Tap or do heart massage on the thymus/heart point and say:

"I acknowledge and release all my sadness and I embrace forgiveness.

Tap under your arms and say:

"I acknowledge and I release any toxic beliefs and/or blocks to once again experiencing a healthy relationship."

Tap under your breasts and say:

"I acknowledge and release any beliefs that I must remain unhappy and alone."

Tap the side of the thumb and say:

"I acknowledge and release any sense of grief or intolerance towards myself or another."

Now tap on the crown of your head and say:

"I acknowledge any anger, grief, or feelings of being punished by the Divine/God/Source, and I trust and know that I am never alone. I know that I deserve to be in a healthy, fulfilling relationship, and I am open to receiving this now."

Now rate your overall progress. Rate your SUDS level in terms of how disturbing or stressful the issue or emotion feels as you once again tune back into your "movie": 0 = no distress/disturbance to 10 = highly stressful/disturbing.

Be gentle with yourself and know that sometimes results are experienced rapidly. However, often persistence may be required to tap away all aspects of an issue. Please contact a professional if your SUDS level goes up or you experience any difficulty with this or any of the other exercises.

After completing three rounds of tapping on the negative issue/emotion, it may be helpful to complete the Nine-Gamut procedure mentioned earlier in Chapter 7.

Also, please refer to the end of this section for an example of Positive Tapping. Positive Tapping is usually completed after approximately three rounds of working on the negative issue/emotion and/or after the Nine-Gamut procedure. The Positive Tapping technique is helpful in affirming what it is you want/choose to replace the negative emotion or issue with.

Tapping for the Death of a Loved One

Tune into your emotions. Try to be as specific as possible. It may be helpful to close your eyes and imagine the aspect of your loss that you want to work on as a movie. This can be a disturbing memory or an emotion.

- Who are the characters?

- What do you hear/see?

- What emotions and/or physical feelings are you experiencing?

Now rate this (SUDS level) in terms of how disturbing or stressful this feels: 0 = no distress/disturbance to 10 = highly stressful/disturbing.

Please be sure to write down this rating in your journal because you will need to refer back to this SUDS level to determine your progress.

Now tap on the Karate Chop or rub the Sore Spots (see Appendix Figure 1) and <u>say aloud three times</u> while tapping/rubbing:

"Even though a part of me feels (name the emotion), I deeply and completely accept this part of me."

Or, *"Even though a part of me continues to remember (disturbing memory), I deeply and completely accept this part me."*

Now tap between your eyebrows and say:

"I acknowledge and release any fear or trauma associated with this loss at its deepest level."

Tap on the side of the eye and say:

"I acknowledge and release any anger or rage associated with this loss at its deepest level."

Tap under both eyes and say:

> *"I acknowledge and I am willing to let go of any anxiety associated with this loss, even at its deepest level."*

Tap under your nose and say:

> *"I acknowledge and release any blocks that would keep me from moving forward with my life."*

Tap under your lower lip and say:

> *"I acknowledge and release any shame or guilt associated with this loss."*

Tap on the collarbone points and say:

> *"I acknowledge and release any feelings of numbness or shock at the deepest level associated with this loss."*

Tap or do heart massage on the thymus/heart point and say:

> *"I acknowledge and release all sadness and sorrow at its deepest level associated with this loss.*

Tap under your arms and say:

> *"I acknowledge and I release any toxic beliefs and/or blocks that may prevent me from recovering."*

Tap under your breasts and say:

> *"I acknowledge and release any beliefs that cause me to believe I must remain unhappy in order to honor the memory of my loved one."*

Tap the side of the thumb and say:

> *"I acknowledge and release the grief associated with the loss of my loved one at its deepest level."*

Now tap on the crown of your head and say:

"I acknowledge any anger, grief, or feelings of being punished by the Divine/God/Source, and I am willing to know that I deserve peace."

Now rate your overall progress. Rate your SUDS level in terms of how disturbing or stressful the issue or emotion feels as you once again tune back into the "movie": 0 = no distress/disturbance to 10 = highly stressful/disturbing.

Be gentle with yourself and know that sometimes results are experienced rapidly; however, often persistence may be required to tap away all aspects of an issue.

Please contact a professional if your SUDS level goes up or you experience any difficulty with this or any of the other exercises.

Note that when dealing with the loss of a loved one, the SUDS level may not reduce to a zero. However, any reduction will assist you in your recovery process.

After completing three rounds of tapping on the negative issue/emotion, it may be helpful to complete the Nine-Gamut procedure mentioned earlier in Chapter 7.

Also, please refer to the end of this section for an example of Positive Tapping. Positive Tapping is usually completed after approximately three rounds of working on the negative issue/emotion, and/or after the Nine-Gamut procedure. The Positive Tapping technique is helpful in affirming what it is you want/choose to replace the negative emotion or issue with.

Tapping for the Loss of a Job/Retirement

Tune into your emotions. Try to be as specific as possible. It may be helpful to close your eyes and imagine the issue you want to work on as a movie:

- Who are the characters?

- What do you hear/see?

- What emotions and/or physical feelings are you experiencing?

Now rate this (SUDS level) in terms of how disturbing or stressful this feels: 0 = no distress/disturbance, to 10 = highly stressful/disturbing. Please be sure to write down this rating in your journal. You will need to refer back to this SUDS level to determine your progress.

Now tap on the Karate Chop or rub the Sore Spots (see Appendix Figure 1) and say aloud three times while tapping/rubbing:

"Even though a part of me feels/believes (name the feeling/belief), I deeply and completely accept this part of me."

Now tap between your eyebrows and say:

"I acknowledge and release any fear or trauma associated with this loss of work."

Tap on the side of the eye and say:

"I acknowledge and release any anger or rage associated with the loss of my job."

Tap under both eyes and say:

"I acknowledge and I am willing to let go of any anxiety associated with the loss of my job and/or my identity."

Tap under your nose and say:

"I acknowledge and release any blocks that would keep me from finding a new job and/or enjoyable activity."

Tap under your lower lip and say:

"I acknowledge and release any shame or guilt associated with the loss of my job or my decision to retire."

Tap on the collarbone points and say:

"I acknowledge and release any feelings of shock related to the loss of my job or my decision to retire."

Tap or do heart massage on the thymus/heart point and say:

"I acknowledge and release all sadness at its deepest level associated with the loss of my job/identity/retirement."

Tap under your arms and say:

"I acknowledge and I release any toxic beliefs and/or blocks that may prevent me from finding another way of supporting myself or enjoying my retirement."

Tap under your breasts and say:

"I acknowledge and release any beliefs that would interfere with my happiness."

Tap the side of the thumb and say:

"I acknowledge and release the grief associated with the loss of my job/retirement."

Now tap on the crown of your head and say:

"I acknowledge any anger, grief, or feelings of being punished by the Divine/God/Source, and I am willing to trust that I will be guided to my highest good."

Now rate your overall progress. Rate your SUDS level in terms of how disturbing or stressful the issue or emotion feels as you once again tune back into the "movie": 0 = no distress/disturbance to 10 = highly stressful/disturbing.

Be gentle with yourself and know that sometimes results are experienced rapidly; however, often persistence may be required to tap away all aspects of an issue. Please contact a professional if your SUDS level goes up or you experience any difficulty with this or any of the other exercises.

After completing three rounds of tapping on the negative issue/emotion, it may be helpful to complete the Nine-Gamut procedure mentioned earlier in Chapter 7.

Also, please refer to the end of this section for an example of Positive Tapping. Positive Tapping is usually completed after approximately three rounds of working on the negative issue/emotion, and/or after the Nine-Gamut procedure. The Positive Tapping technique is helpful in affirming what it is you want/choose to replace the negative emotion or issue with.

Tapping for the Loss of Status/Life Style

Tune into your emotions, issue, or problem. Try to be as specific as possible. It may be helpful to close your eyes and imagine the issue you want to work on as a movie:

- Who are the characters?

- What do you hear/see?

- What emotions and/or physical feelings are you experiencing?

Now rate this (SUDS level) in terms of how disturbing or stressful this feels: 0 = no distress/disturbance to 10 = highly stressful/disturbing. Please be sure to write down this rating in your journal; you will need to refer back to this SUDS level to determine your progress.

Now tap on the Karate Chop or rub the Sore Spots (see Appendix Figure 1) and say aloud three times while tapping/rubbing:

"Even though a part of me has this issue (name the problem/issue), I deeply and completely accept this part of me."

Or, if you are experiencing a strong emotion attached to this loss, use the following phrase:

"Even though a part of me feels (name the feeling/emotion), I deeply and completely accept this part of me."

Now tap between your eyebrows and say:

"I acknowledge and release any fear or trauma associated with this loss at its deepest level."

Tap on the side of the eye and say:

"I acknowledge and release any anger or rage associated with this loss at its deepest level."

Tap under both eyes and say:

"I acknowledge and I am willing to let go of any anxiety associated with this loss, even at its deepest level."

Tap under your nose and say:

"I acknowledge and release any blocks that would keep me from moving forward with my life."

Tap under your lower lip and say:

"I acknowledge and release any shame or guilt associated with this loss."

Tap on the collarbone points and say:

"I acknowledge and release any feelings of numbness or shock at the deepest level associated with this loss."

Tap or do heart massage on the thymus/heart point and say:

"I acknowledge and release all sadness and sorrow at its deepest level associated with this loss."

Tap under your arms and say:

"I acknowledge and I release any toxic beliefs and/or blocks that may prevent me from recovering."

Tap under your breasts and say:

"I acknowledge and release any beliefs that would interfere with my happiness."

Tap the side of the thumb and say:

"I acknowledge and release the grief associated with the loss of my life style at its deepest level."

Now tap on the crown of your head and say:

"I acknowledge any anger, grief, or feelings of being punished by the Divine/God/Source, and I am willing to trust that my life/status will continue to improve once again."

Now rate your overall progress. Rate your SUDS level in terms of how disturbing or stressful the issue or emotion feels as you once again tune back into the "movie": 0 = no distress/disturbance to 10 = highly stressful/disturbing.

Be gentle with yourself and know that sometimes results are experienced rapidly; however, often persistence may be required to tap away all aspects of an issue.

Please contact a professional if your SUDS level goes up or you experience any difficulty with this or any of the other exercises.

After completing three rounds of tapping on the negative issue/emotion, it may be helpful to complete the Nine-Gamut procedure mentioned earlier in Chapter 7.

Also, please refer to the end of this section for an example of Positive Tapping. Positive Tapping is usually completed after approximately three rounds of working on the negative issue/emotion, and/or after the Nine-Gamut procedure. The Positive Tapping technique is helpful in affirming what it is you want/choose to replace the negative emotion or issue with.

Tapping for the Loss of Faith &/or Divine Homesickness

Tune into your emotions. Try to be as specific as possible. It may be helpful to close your eyes and imagine the issue you want to work on as a movie:

- Who are the characters?

- What do you hear/see?

- What emotions and/or physical feelings are you experiencing?

Now rate this (SUDS level) in terms of how disturbing or stressful this feels: 0 = no distress/disturbance to 10 = highly stressful/disturbing. Please be sure and write down this rating in your journal; you will need to refer back to this SUDS level to determine your progress.

Now tap on the Karate Chop or rub the Sore Spots (see Appendix Figure 1) and say out loud three times while tapping/rubbing:

"Even though a part of me has lost my faith, I deeply and completely accept this part of me."

and/or

"Even though a part of me feels abandoned by God/Source/the Divine, I deeply and completely accept this part of me."

Now tap between your eyebrows and say:

"I acknowledge and release any fear or trauma associated with this loss of faith &/or feelings of abandonment."

Tap on the side of the eye and say:

"I acknowledge and release any anger or rage associated with the loss of my faith &/or feelings of abandonment."

Tap under both eyes and say:

"I acknowledge and I am willing to let go of any anxiety associated with the loss of my faith &/or feelings of abandonment."

Tap under your nose and say:

"I acknowledge and release any blocks that would keep me from rebuilding my faith &/or feeling connected to God."

Tap under your lower lip and say:

"I acknowledge and release any shame or guilt associated with losing my faith &/or having inappropriate relationships."

Tap on the collarbone points and say:

"I acknowledge and release any feelings of shock and disappointment related to God and my loss of faith &/or feeling abandoned."

Tap or do heart massage on the thymus/heart point and say:

"I acknowledge and release all sadness at its deepest level associated with my loss of faith &/or feelings of Divine Homesickness."

Tap under your arms and say:

"I acknowledge and I release any toxic beliefs and/or blocks that may prevent me from finding a way to renew my faith &/or stay fully present in my life.

Tap under your breasts and say:

"I acknowledge and release any beliefs that would interfere with my connecting with the Divine (God) once again."

Tap the side of the thumb and say:

"I acknowledge and release the grief associated with my loss of faith &/or feelings of Divine Homesickness."

Now tap on the crown of your head and say:

"I acknowledge any feelings of being punished, anger, grief, or disappointment in the Divine (God/Source), and I willing trust and renew my faith in God/Source/the Divine once again."

Now rate your overall progress. Rate your SUDS level in terms of how disturbing or stressful this issue or emotion feels as you once again tune back into the "movie": 0 = no distress/disturbance to 10 = highly stressful/disturbing.

Be gentle with yourself and know that sometimes results are experienced rapidly; however, often persistence may be required to tap away all aspects of an issue.

Please contact a professional if your SUDS level goes up or you experience any difficulty with this or any of the other exercises.

After completing three rounds of tapping on the negative issue/emotion, it may be helpful to complete the Nine-Gamut procedure mentioned earlier in Chapter 7.

Also, please refer to the end of this section for an example of Positive Tapping. Positive Tapping is usually completed after approximately three rounds of working on the negative issue/emotion, and/or after the Nine-Gamut procedure. The Positive Tapping technique is helpful in affirming what it is you want/choose to replace the negative emotion or issue with.

Tapping for the Loss of Ability/Mobility

Tune into your emotions, issue, or problem. Try to be as specific as possible. It may be helpful to close your eyes and imagine the issue you want to work on as a movie:

- Who are the characters?

- What do you hear/see?

- What emotions and/or physical feelings are you experiencing?

Now rate this (SUDS level) in terms of how disturbing or stressful this feels: 0 = no distress/disturbance to 10 = highly stressful/disturbing. Please be sure and write down this rating in your journal; you will need to refer back to this SUDS level to determine your progress.

Now tap on the Karate Chop or rub the Sore Spots (see Appendix Figure 1) and say aloud three times while tapping/rubbing:

"Even though a part of me has this issue (name the problem/issue), I deeply and completely accept this part of me."

Or, if you are experiencing a strong emotion attached to this loss, use the following phrase:

"Even though a part of me feels (name the feeling/emotion), I deeply and completely accept this part of me."

*You may use the general term ability/mobility, but remember: the more specific, the better.

Now tap between your eyebrows and say:

"I acknowledge and release any fear or trauma associated with this loss of ability/mobility (name the loss, i.e., ability to walk) at its deepest level."

Tap on the side of the eye and say:

"I acknowledge and release any anger or rage associated with this loss of ability/mobility (name the loss) at its deepest level."

Tap under both eyes and say:

"I acknowledge and I am willing to let go of any anxiety associated with this loss of ability/mobility (name the loss), even at its deepest level."

Tap under your nose and say:

"I acknowledge and release any blocks that would keep me from moving forward with my life, even with this loss of (name the loss) ability/mobility."

Tap under your lower lip and say:

"I acknowledge and release any shame or guilt associated with this loss of (name the loss) ability/mobility."

Tap on the collarbone points and say:

"I acknowledge and release any feelings of numbness or shock at the deepest level associated with this loss of (name the loss) ability/mobility."

Tap or do heart massage on the thymus/heart point and say:

"I acknowledge and release all sadness and sorrow at its deepest level associated with this loss of (name the loss) ability/mobility."

Tap under your arms and say:

"I acknowledge and I release any toxic beliefs and/or blocks that may prevent me from recovering from my loss of (name the loss) ability/mobility."

Tap under your breasts and say:

"I acknowledge and release any beliefs that cause me to believe I must remain unhappy because of my loss of (name the loss) ability/mobility."

Tap the side of the thumb and say:

"I acknowledge and release the grief associated with the loss of (name the loss) ability/mobility at its deepest level."

Now tap on the crown of your head and say:

"I acknowledge any anger, grief, or feelings of being punished by the Divine/God/Source, and I am willing to know that I deserve peace in spite of my loss of (name the loss) ability/mobility."

Now rate your overall progress. Rate your SUDS level in terms of how disturbing or stressful the issue or emotion feels as you once again tune back into the "movie": 0 = no distress/disturbance to 10 = highly stressful/disturbing.

Please contact a professional if your SUDS level goes up, or you experience any difficulty with this or any of the other exercises in this book.

Remember: the more specific, the better. For example, if you have lost your ability to speak, use this in place of "ability/mobility" within the above phrases. Be gentle with yourself and know that sometimes results are experienced rapidly; however, often persistence may be required to tap away all aspects of an issue. After completing three rounds of tapping on the negative issue/emotion, it may be helpful to complete the Nine-Gamut procedure mentioned earlier in Chapter 7.

Also, please refer to the end of this section for an example of Positive Tapping. Positive Tapping is usually completed after approximately three rounds of working on the negative issue/emotion and/or after the Nine-Gamut procedure. The

Positive Tapping technique is helpful in affirming what it is you want/choose to replace the negative emotion or issue with.

Positive Tapping Statement

Now that you have tapped on the negative aspects of an issue, it can be helpful to go through the points and tap on what you want/choose to replace the negative aspects with—often, this is the exact opposite of the negative aspect. The following script is an example of tapping on the positive. Please remember, the more specific, the better, so, as always, feel free to add your own words to this exercise.

Now tap on the Karate Chop or rub the Sore Spots (see Appendix Figure 1) and say aloud three times while tapping/rubbing:

*"Even though a part of me **had** this (name the problem/issue/feeling), I deeply and completely accept this part of me, and I choose (forgiveness, happiness, etc.)."*

Now tap between your eyebrows and say:

"I see beyond any fear and know this fear is an illusion. I see clearly now."

Tap on the side of the eye and say:

"I release any remaining anger and begin forgiving myself and others now. I embrace tolerance now."

Tap under both eyes and say:

"I am willing to let go so that I may receive; I am open to receive my highest good now."

Tap under your nose and say:

"I release any remaining blocks and move forward with ease now."

Tap under your lower lip and say:

"I release any shame or guilt and claim all my power back now."

Tap on the collarbone points and say:

"I release any remaining feelings of shock, and I am free to feel good once again."

Tap or do heart massage on the thymus/heart point and say:

"I forgive myself and love myself unconditionally. I am open to experiencing love once again."

Tap under your arms and say:

"I replace any toxic beliefs with positive affirmations." (Go ahead and insert any positive affirmations you would like now.)

Tap under your breasts and say:

"I choose to be happy once again."

Tap the side of the thumb and say:

"I find tolerance and joy within myself once again."

Now tap on the crown of your head and say:

"I trust that I am connected and being guided by the Divine now and always; I am open to receiving this guidance and unconditional love once again."

Appendix B:
Recommended Reading and References

Achterberg, J., Dossey, B. & Kolkmeier, L. (1994). *Rituals of Healing: Using Imagery for Health and Wellness*. New York, NY: Bantam Books.

Bender, S. & Sise, M. (2007). *The Energy of Belief: Psychology's Power Tools to Focus Intention and Release Blocking Beliefs*. Santa Rosa, CA: Energy Psychology Press.

Bowers, D.T. (2005). *Guiding Your Family Through Loss and Grief*. Tucson, AZ: Fenestra Books.

Braden, G. (2007). *The Divine Matrix: Bridging Time, Space, Miracles, and Belief*. Carlsbad, CA: Hay House, Inc.

Brennan, B. (1987). *Hands of Light*. New York: Bantam.

Canfield, J. & Bruner, P. (2012). *Tapping Into Ultimate Success: How to Overcome Any Obstacle and Skyrocket Your Results*. Carlsbad, CA: Hay House, Inc.

Carrington, P. (2008). *Discover the Power of Meridian Tapping: A Revolutionary Method for Stress-Free Living*. Bethel, CT: Try It Productions.

Christman, Y. (2002). Subtle Energy Healing A Clinical Approach. Tools for Conscious Change & The Wellness Institute Training.

Childre, D. L. & Martin, H. (1999). *The HeartMath Solution: The Institute of HeartMath's Revolutionary Program for Engaging the Power of the Heart's Intelligence*. New York. NY: Harper Collins Publishers.

Eden, D. (with Feinstein, D.) (1999). *Energy Medicine*. New York, NY: Tarcher/Penquin Putnam.

Encarta Dictionary: English North America (online resource).

Feinstein, D. (2008). Energy Psychology in Disaster Relief. *Traumatology*. 14(*1*), 124-137.

Feinstein, D. (2004). *Energy Psychology Interactive: Rapid Interventions for Lasting Change*. Canada: Innersource.

Gallo, F. (2007). *Energy Tapping for Trauma: Rapid Relief from Post-Traumatic Stress Using Energy Psychology*. Oakland, CA: New Harbinger Publications.

Gerber, R. (2001). *Vibrational Medicine: The #1 Handbook of Subtle-Energy Therapies. (3ʳᵈ ed.)*. Rochester, Vermont: Bear & Company.

Hover-Kramer, D. (2002). *Creative Energies: Integrative Energy Psychotherapy for Self-Expression and Healing*. New York, NY: W.W. Norton & Company.

Killgore, M. (2008). *Who Am I? How Do I Find Me?* Meda Killgore, 124 Killgore Rd. Ruston, LA 71270.

Muller, B. (2011). *Energy Makeover: A Conscious Way to Stay Young, Have Fun and Get More Done*. Motivational Press.

McTaggert, L. (2007). *The Intention Experiment: Using Your Thoughts to Change Your Life and the World*. New York, NY: Free Press.

McTaggert, L. (2002). *The Field: The Quest for the Secret Force of the Universe*. New York, NY: Harper Collins Publishers Inc.

Pert, C. (1997). *Molecules of Emotion: Why You Feel the Way You Feel*. New York, NY: Scribener.

Schupp, L. J. (2007). *Grief: Normal, Complicated, Traumatic*. Eau Claire, Wisconsin: PESI Healthcare, LLC.

Stone, B. (2008). *Invisible Roots: How Healing Past Life Trauma Can Liberate Your Present.* Santa Rosa, CA: Energy Psychology Press.

Tarlow, M. (1999). *Navigating the Future: A Personal Guide to Achieving Success in the New Millennium.* New York, NY: McGraw-Hill.

Worden, J.W. (2009). *Grief Counseling & Grief Therapy: A Handbook for the Mental Health Practitioner.* New York, NY: Springer Publishing Company.

Wright, H. N. (2009). *Recovering from Losses in Life.* Grand Rapids, MI: Revell Publishing.

Appendix C:
Eden's Routine and Labyrinth

Donna Eden's Five Minute Daily Routine
(Based on Donna Eden's Daily Energy Routine)

The Hook Up: Centers Energy

- Place the middle finger of one hand just above the nose.

- Place the middle finger of the other hand in the belly button

- Hold and pull up slightly for about 1-3 minutes.

•· Switch hands & repeat.

Three Thumps: Increases Energy & Strengthens Immune System

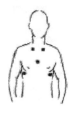

- With fingertips and thumb, massage/tap points shown in picture.

- Breathe deeply at each point.

Cross Crawl: Balances Energies & Clears Thinking

- March in place in this way:
- Lift right arm & left leg simultaneously.
- Next lift left arm & right leg.
- Repeat at least 12 to 20 times.

Figure Eights: Strengthens & Crosses Energy

- Make figure 8 patterns in front & on sides with both hands & arms.
- Use a swinging motion making small and/or large figure 8 patterns.

Wayne Cook Posture: Unscrambles Energy, Calms, & Clears Thinking

- Sit on edge of chair & place ankle on top of left knee.
- Place left hand on top of ankle.
- Wrap right hand around ball of the foot—take 5-7 deep breaths.

- Repeat same posture for other side.

- Uncross legs, place thumb & finger tips together and place above bridge of nose.
- Take 2 deep breaths.

Crown Pull: Clears the Mind & Calms Nervous System

- Bring both hands to forehead, placing fingertips on center of forehead just above eyebrows.

- With gentle pressure, pull fingers apart toward hairline

- Repeat this all the way to back of head & down to bottom of hairline.

- Next place hands on shoulders & gently pull forward, letting hands fall.

Separating Heaven & Earth: Creates Space in Joints

- Stand with hands on thighs, fingers spread, & take a deep breath.

- Bring your arms up above your head and then into prayer position.

- Inhale through your nose. Stretch one arm up & one down.

- Pushing with your palms, turn head/neck facing the side of the raised arm—hold 5+ seconds.

- Switch sides and repeat 5 times.

- Drop arms down and bend forward at the waist.

- Relax with knees slightly bent.

- Take a few deep breaths (also you can do figure 8s if you wish) and slowly return to standing position.

Zip Up: Increases Confidence, Self-Protection, & Clears Thinking

- Rub hands together & shake off.

- Using hands or fingertips, trace from the top of your pubic bone to lower lip 2-3 times.

- Now trace from the tail bone over the head to your upper lip 2-3 times.

- Imagine locking in this energy pattern after completing each side (front and back) with an imaginary key.

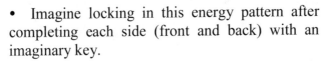

Appendix C: Eden's Routine and Labyrinth

Figure 10.1 Labyrinth

Appendix D:
Recommended Websites

www.energypsych.org (Association for Comprehensive Energy Psychology).

www.mindbodyspirit-innergrations.com (Author's website)

www.LearnEnergyMedicine.com. (Donna Eden's Innersource website for Energy Medicine).

www.EnergyPsychologyResearch.com (Feinstein's Energy Psychology: Method, Theory & Evidence).

http://noosphere.princeton.edu/ (The Global Consciousness Project)

www.energymed.org (handout bank—Six Pillars of Energy Medicine, D. Feinstein, & D. Eden).

Recommended CDs & MP3s

A Meditation to Transform Your Inner Critic by Sherry O'Brian, LCSW, NBCCHt, DCEP.

Release & Transform Burden: a meditation to awaken the healing light within by Sherry O'Brian, LCSW, ACHT, DCEP.

Live ON EARTH (For a Limited Time Only), by Krishna Das (Chanting CD).

Door of Faith by Krishna Das (Chanting CD).

Songs of the Spirit Volume 1-4 by Karen Drucker (Chanting CD).

The Divine Name: Sounds of the God Code by Gregg Braden and Jonathan Goldman.

Sherry has a gift for you!

If you purchase this book, please visit Sherry's author page @ http://www.ozarkmt.com/ and receive your free download of *A Meditation to Transform Your Inner Critic*. Just use the code "Transform."

About the Author

Sherry O'Brian is a psychotherapist who has assisted thousands of individuals through her workshops, groups, and private practice to transform their pain into possibility. The inspiration behind *Peaks and Valleys: Integrative Approaches for Recovering from Loss* is her passion to provide a larger audience with these transformational tools. Sherry has also developed a meditation CD, *Release and Transform Burden: a meditation to awaken the healing light within*, as well as *A Meditation to Transform Your Inner Critic* to assist others with releasing emotional pain and transforming their lives. These meditations are shared in this book and are available on her website: www.mindbodyspirit-innergrations.com.

Sherry is the sole proprietor of Mind/Body/Spirit Inner-grations and specializes in personal growth and transformation, as well as working with those suffering from chronic illness, grief/loss, and other emotional disorders. She also facilitates support groups for cancer patients and their family members at The Cancer Support Community of Central Indiana, as well as develops seminars and workshops on mind/body/spirit healing as an independent contractor for several professional organizations.

As a motivational speaker her workshops and retreats focus on mind/body/spirit healing and personal growth. Sherry has presented several times at the Association for Comprehensive Energy Psychology, The International Society for the Study of Subtle Energies and Energy Medicine, and the National Association of Social Workers conferences, sharing innovative, often cutting-edge techniques, to inspire, motivate, and empower other professionals to better assist their clients.

Sherry has over fifteen years experience in the oncology field, as well as nineteen years within the field of mental health. She is certified in Comprehensive Energy Psychology, Emotional Freedom Technique, Advanced Clinical Hypnotherapy, Psych-K™, Subtle Energy Therapy, Bereavement Counseling, & Guided Imagery. She is a Reiki Master and an ordained minister.

She is a member of the National Board for Certified Clinical Hypnotherapist, Association for Comprehensive Energy Psychology, National Association of Social Workers, Heart-Centered Therapies Association, & The International Society for the Study of Subtle Energies and Energy Medicine. She is a graduate of Butler University, Indiana University Kokomo, & Indiana University School of Social Work.

Other Books By Ozark Mountain Publishing, Inc.

Dolores Cannon
Conversations with Nostradamus,
 Volume I, II, III
Jesus and the Essenes
They Walked with Jesus
Between Death and Life
A Soul Remembers Hiroshima
Keepers of the Garden.
The Legend of Starcrash
The Custodians
The Convoluted Universe - Book One,
 Two, Three, Four
Five Lives Remembered
The Three Waves of Volunteers and the
 New Earth
Stuart Wilson & Joanna Prentis
The Essenes - Children of the Light
Power of the Magdalene
Beyond Limitations
Atlantis and the New Consciousness
The Magdalene Version
O.T. Bonnett, M.D./Greg Satre
Reincarnation: The View from Eternity
What I Learned After Medical School
Why Healing Happens
M. Don Schorn
Elder Gods of Antiquity
Legacy of the Elder Gods
Gardens of the Elder Gods
Reincarnation...Stepping Stones of Life
Aron Abrahamsen
Holiday in Heaven
Out of the Archives – Earth Changes
Sherri Cortland
Windows of Opportunity
Raising Our Vibrations for the New Age
The Spiritual Toolbox
Michael Dennis
Morning Coffee with God
God's Many Mansions
Nikki Pattillo
Children of the Stars
A Spiritual Evolution
Rev. Grant H. Pealer
Worlds Beyond Death
A Funny Thing Happened on the Way to
 Heaven
Maiya & Geoff Gray-Cobb
Angels - The Guardians of Your Destiny
Maiya Gray-Cobb
Seeds of the Soul
Sture Lönnerstrand
I Have Lived Before
Arun & Sunanda Gandhi
The Forgotten Woman
Claire Doyle Beland
Luck Doesn't Happen by Chance

James H. Kent
Past Life Memories As A Confederate
 Soldier
Dorothy Leon
Is Jehovah An E.T
Justine Alessi & M. E. McMillan
Rebirth of the Oracle
Donald L. Hicks
The Divinity Factor
Christine Ramos, RN
A Journey Into Being
Mary Letorney
Discover The Universe Within You
Debra Rayburn
Let's Get Natural With Herbs
Jodi Felice
The Enchanted Garden
Susan Mack & Natalia Krawetz
My Teachers Wear Fur Coats
Ronald Chapman
Seeing True
Rev. Keith Bender
The Despiritualized Church
Vara Humphreys
The Science of Knowledge
Karen Peebles
The Other Side of Suicide
Antoinette Lee Howard
Journey Through Fear
Julia Hanson
Awakening To Your Creation
Irene Lucas
Thirty Miracles in Thirty Days
Mandeep Khera
Why?
Robert Winterhalter
The Healing Christ
James Wawro
Ask Your Inner Voice
Tom Arbino
You Were Destined to be Together
Maureen McGill & Nola Davis
Live From the Other Side
Anita Holmes
TWIDDERS
Walter Pullen
Evolution of the Spirit
Cinnamon Crow
Teen Oracle
Chakra Zodiac Healing Oracle
Jack Churchward
Lifting the Veil on the Lost Continent of
 Mu

For more information about any of the above titles, soon to be released titles,
or other items in our catalog, write or visit our website:
PO Box 754, Huntsville, AR 72740
www.ozarkmt.com

Other Books By Ozark Mountain Publishing, Inc.

Guy Needler
The History of God
Beyond the Source – Book 1,2
Dee Wallace/Jarred Hewett
The Big E
Dee Wallace
Conscious Creation
Natalie Sudman
Application of Impossible Things
Henry Michaelson
And Jesus Said – A Conversation
Victoria Pendragon
SleepMagic
Riet Okken
The Liberating Power of Emotions
Janie Wells
Payment for Passage
Dennis Wheatley/ Maria Wheatley
The Essential Dowsing Guide
Dennis Milner
Kosmos
Garnet Schulhauser
Dancing on a Stamp
Julia Cannon
Soul Speak – The Language of Your
    Body
Charmian Redwood
Coming Home to Lemuria
Kathryn Andries
Soul Choices – 6 Paths to Find Your Life
    Purpose

For more information about any of the above titles, soon to be released titles,
or other items in our catalog, write or visit our website:
PO Box 754, Huntsville, AR 72740
www.ozarkmt.com